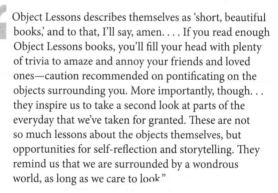

The Object Lessons series achieves something very close to magic: the books take ordinary—even banal—objects and animate them with a rich history of invention, political struggle, science, and popular mythology. Filled with fascinating details and conveyed in sharp, accessible prose, the books make the everyday world come to life. Be warned: once you've read a few of these, you'll start walking around your house, picking up random objects, and musing aloud: 'I wonder what the story is behind this thing?'"

Steven Johnson, **author of** *Where Good Ideas Come From* **and** *How We Got to Now*

Object Lessons describes themselves as 'short, beautiful books,' and to that, I'll say, amen. . . . If you read enough Object Lessons books, you'll fill your head with plenty of trivia to amaze and annoy your friends and loved ones—caution recommended on pontificating on the objects surrounding you. More importantly, though. . . they inspire us to take a second look at parts of the everyday that we've taken for granted. These are not so much lessons about the objects themselves, but opportunities for self-reflection and storytelling. They remind us that we are surrounded by a wondrous world, as long as we care to look"

ribune

T0205070

"For my money, Object Lessons is the most consistently interesting nonfiction book series in America."

Megan Volpert, *PopMatters*

"Besides being beautiful little hand-sized objects themselves, showcasing exceptional writing, the wonder of these books is that they exist at all . . . Uniformly excellent, engaging, thought-provoking, and informative."

Jennifer Bort Yacovissi, *Washington Independent Review of Books*

". . . edifying and entertaining . . . perfect for slipping in a pocket and pulling out when life is on hold."

Sarah Murdoch, *Toronto Star*

"[W]itty, thought-provoking, and poetic . . . These little books are a page-flipper's dream."

John Timpane, *The Philadelphia Inquirer*

"Though short, at roughly 25,000 words apiece, these books are anything but slight."

Marina Benjamin, *New Statesman*

OBJECT LESSONS

A book series about the hidden lives of ordinary things.

Series Editors:

Ian Bogost and Christopher Schaberg

Advisory Board:

Sara Ahmed, Jane Bennett, Jeffrey Jerome Cohen, Johanna Drucker, Raiford Guins, Graham Harman, renée hoogland, Pam Houston, Eileen Joy, Douglas Kahn, Daniel Miller, Esther Milne, Timothy Morton, Kathleen Stewart, Nigel Thrift, Rob Walker, Michele White.

In association with

LOYOLA
UNIVERSITY
NEW ORLEANS

Georgia | Center for
Tech | Media Studies

BOOKS IN THE SERIES

sticker

HENRY HOKE

BLOOMSBURY ACADEMIC
NEW YORK • LONDON • OXFORD • NEW DELHI • SYDNEY

BLOOMSBURY ACADEMIC
Bloomsbury Publishing Inc
1385 Broadway, New York, NY 10018, USA
50 Bedford Square, London, WC1B 3DP, UK
29 Earlsfort Terrace, Dublin 2, Ireland

BLOOMSBURY, BLOOMSBURY ACADEMIC and the Diana logo are trademarks
of Bloomsbury Publishing Plc

First published in the United States of America 2022

Copyright © Henry Hoke, 2022

Cover design: Alice Marwick

A catalog record for this book is available from the Library of Congress.

ISBN: PB: 978-1-5013-6722-9
ePDF: 978-1-5013-6724-3
eBook: 978-1-5013-6723-6

Series: Object Lessons

Typeset by Deanta Global Publishing Services, Chennai, India
Printed and bound in the United States of America

To find out more about our authors and books visit www.bloomsbury.com and sign
up for our newsletters.

CONTENTS

MR. YUK

Mr. Yuk was my first crush.

His face dotted the containers in the underbelly of the kitchen sink. His tongue protruded from the upper shelves of the medicine cabinet, taunting me. Mr. Yuk was famous. He even had his own theme song that'd play on PBS between shows:

Mr. Yuk is mean
Mr. Yuk is green

"We don't touch if we see Mr. Yuk," warned Mom.

This sticker wielded a dark power.

The doctor that designed Mr. Yuk had an altruistic mission: to prevent accidental poisonings with a universal symbol that the smallest of children could register as bad, a color that any kid would find repellant. The skull-and-crossbones wasn't working anymore: pirates were all a kid could ever want to be and the bottles their symbol adorned were inviting to ingest. As soon as my little brother was old enough to pick out his own clothes, he would drape himself in a dress-sized T-shirt that was fully covered in photo-realistic skulls. In Pittsburgh—where Mr. Yuk was invented—the Pirates were the major league baseball team. A kid could mistake toxic substances for sports juice, the skull-and-crossbones an endorsement. *Drink me.*

The focus group used to choose Mr. Yuk's details was composed of the potentially poisoned themselves, some 70s Pennsylvania tykes. Dr. Richard Moriarty and an ad agency subjected them to various designs, to find out what they were drawn to, what alarmed them. They were asked what happens if they messed with poison: "Your mother will yell at you," they responded. "You'll get sick, you'll die." When given a range of options, they chose the sick face over the yelling face or the dead face.[1] Yuk had to be a Mister. Their mothers were the ones looking out for them. All the man of the house could do was register repulsion.

So, Mr. Yuk, this nemesis of smiley face—eyebrows knit in pain, nauseated tongue extended—was born in fluorescent green, and stuck. A new icon. Today on the University of Pittsburgh Medical Center website I can buy a sexy pink T-shirt emblazoned with my old crush. It promises to be, "incredibly soft with great drape."

Get to know his face
in every single place

The same year that Mr. Yuk was introduced, 1971, a children's book series called *Mr. Men* arrived. Simple and colorful, the Mr. Men were named for their one defining attribute: the yellow Mr. Happy, the fat pink Mr. Greedy, the squiggly pink Mr. Messy.

I was born twelve years later and was immediately gifted these colorful *Mr.* books. In my developing brain, Mr. Yuk was one of the Mr. Men crew, and by far the best. The Mr. Men in the books couldn't be removed—they stayed flat and unstickable, confined to their covers. But Mr. Yuk was everywhere. I'd seen Mom with a whole roll of Mr. Yuks to peel and place on bottle after bottle, and I knew that this roll was still lurking somewhere in the house.

Home is full of bad things
that can hurt you very much

Dr. Moriarty and his team speculated that kids might not really pay attention to the sticker, but that the act of stickering would make parents more cautious about the toxic products in their house, where and how they stored them and kept them from teeny hands and growing throats.

I learned early to open the safety latch on the cabinet below the sink. I'd take out a bottle of whatever deadly liquid and gaze at Mr. Yuk. He held the forbidden behind his grimace. I saw a reflection of my own face, my own disgust mirrored. I'd knit my eyebrows just so.

I fuck with Mr. Yuk, I thought, but didn't think, because children don't think "fuck" and "fuck with" wasn't a phrase yet, but the feeling was there. That feeling drew me closer and closer to danger every little day.

If Mr. Yuk was a scratch-and-sniff, he'd smell like death-wish.

UNICORN

The first time I heard the word "gay" I closed my open palm and drew my arm back to clutch my chest. It was snack time in second grade and Ponytail had a sheet of sparkling unicorn stickers to give out. She gave them to all the girls, then sat at her desk in front of me and swiveled around with one remaining. I held out my hand and Blonde Boy said the word, shoving my desire back where it lived.

I was jealous of the opulence available to the girls. Lisa Frank had exploded and the rainbows and animals of her designs covered me in their glow from the backpacks, folders and pencil cases of my female classmates. My pink stickers had to be private, pushed up onto the upper roof of the inside of my desk, where I could finger the glitter and carry some with me. Where Blonde Boy couldn't see.

Blonde Boy was the most boy of anyone in class. "If you give me a pencil, I'll give you a baby," he'd bark at girls before any of us understood what was funny or wrong in that. Blonde Boy and I had a sadomasochistic relationship: he'd punch me in the shoulder every chance he got, but it didn't stop me from sitting next to him; my hair was a depository for his chewed gum. He was my best friend.

If a unicorn was a scratch-and-sniff it'd smell like Ponytail.

Ponytail's ponytail was the longest in class and it whipped across my field of vision all day. She and Blonde Boy seemed like sworn members of rival clans, their hate for each other fundamental beyond the gender divide. "Unicorns go to gay hell," Blonde Boy declared at recess. "Yeah," I agreed. Then he gave me a job.

Recess ended and we were back to our teacher's math drone. Subtraction, probably. Each grade at the elementary school had its own floor of the building. We ascended every year, kindergarten through fourth, ground floor on up. We'd reached the treetops. To my left I could see the earliest dying leaves. To my right Blonde Boy blew spitballs at me, daring me to do the thing. When I looked at him, he nodded. I lifted my safety scissors, cut off Ponytail's ponytail and stuffed it in my desk.

A week later we took a field trip to the local dairy farm. Our bus parked near a huge barn and everyone filed off. Transfixed by the bored cows, I broke from the group and walked toward the pasture. Lisa Frank's rainbow fantasy imagination—an imagination that wormed its way into my everyday longing—extended past mythic beasts and patterned jungle cats to the mundane: a cool cow. Her cool cow, printed on stickers and stretched across folders, had rainbow sunglasses and purple spots. I saw the herd in this light, imagined them sporting flowery jam shorts, lipstick and single earrings. The pasture was vibrant in my augmented vision.

If a cow was a scratch-and-sniff it'd smell like shit.

I grabbed onto the fence in front of me. Something heavy slammed into my body, from my butt up to my brain. It felt as if I'd been kicked in the ass incredibly hard. I let go of the electrified fence, reeling from the shock and oblivious of the cause, whipped around to see who had hurt me. My classmates were at least ten yards away. But Blonde Boy was closest. I knew in my heart he was the kicker.

I roared and ran at Blonde Boy, tackling him to the ground. I closed my open palm to punch but our teacher pulled me off, my body still trembling with electric current. Blonde Boy lay in the mud and gravel, smiling. We didn't talk again until I had forgotten his name.

WAHOOWA

Responses, 1998-2018, when I tell a stranger or near-stranger that I'm from Charlottesville:

> *Uh-huh.*
> *So you're like, Southern.*
> *Is that near DC? That's the only Virginia I've been to.*
> *Okay.*
> *I thought that was North Carolina.*
> *Oh yeah. I love Dave.*
> *Where?*
> *Cool, my mom's family is from Lynchburg.*
> *. . . great.*
> *I've been, just to tour the college. Thomas Jefferson.*
> *Go Hornets.*
> *Oh, it's so beautiful there.*
> *Do you know Dave?*
> *My uncle lives in Raleigh.*
> *But you don't have an accent.*
> *I know, you told me already. I have no idea where that is.*

*Totally. Go Hoos. My dad went to UVA. He's got a sticker
on his car: Wahoowa. That's totally the best mascot. The
fish. Dad says the wahoo fish doesn't know when to stop
drinking, so it just keeps drinking until it explodes.*

Oh.

Fuck.

You weren't there, though, right?

Anyway,

I'm sorry.

*That's a brave thing to advertise. But I'm sure it's a nice
place. Only it's got some people in it with some very bad
ideas.*

Oh.

Thank god you got out.

GOLD STAR

Gold stars ruined our education.

The charts were there on the wall from the beginning—lined graphs with each of our names running down the left side, empty and unassuming. Then they began to fill. Whenever we did something listed on the chart, something as simple as eating every bite of our lunch or placing our mat back in the cubby area after naptime, the teacher stuck a star in the corresponding box. The stars rested in the teacher's desk, and we longed for their continued accrual. The stars became a galactic footrace, their sparkle visible from the furthest corners of the room, everyone's progress glaring. We knew at all times who was racking them up and who was trailing behind. We learned lack. This wasn't a childhood anymore, but a burgeoning assessment. A competition that would never end.

My first grade year at Venable Elementary—one of five public K-4 schools in Charlottesville, Virginia—we were sent to a different building while the city did extensive renovations to the original school. Venable was nestled in the center of a residential neighborhood, across from trees and houses. Its grand staircase, red brick, and tall white columns mimicked the Jeffersonian architecture of the University of Virginia Grounds, less than a mile down the street.

The "swing school" we spent that renovation year attending was more generic and looked like any other school in town: two long stories of brick, doors, windows, forgettable in relation to the grandiosity we'd come from. It was called Jefferson, and sat a block off West Main Street near downtown, across from the parking lot of a big-box store. Its gymnasium was a community recreation center, but the school section felt as if it had been out of use for a while. We settled in with our teacher Ms. Perfume, not minding the change, and spent a fall, a winter, and a spring in its classrooms and on its small square playground overlooking the city. I remember seeing my first outie belly button, when a kid pulled up his shirt to waggle it around.

The gold stars stayed with us and became inconsistent. Ms. Perfume plastered one to a story I wrote, and next to the star, in red cursive, she scribbled, "You are a very sick person!" The story was a violent showdown called "Butt Kickin' Time," a detail Mom won't let me forget, because she probably had to have a meeting with the teacher about it to make sure everything was okay in my bloody little mind. I didn't witness this meeting. All I got was encouragement, more stars. Attendance is attendance and gets gold, even if a boy is a nightmare the whole time.

With the summer after first grade behind us, we returned to Venable Elementary, polished and refurbished inside, the splintering wooden playground structure replaced with shiny plastic tubes and soft shredded-rubber turf. The new look called for a new school mascot, and the administration decided to let us students choose our own identity. Every kid got to write in a possibility. The Venable Ladybugs. The Venable Vampires. Mom jokes that I most likely lobbied for The Venable Butt-Kickers, but I don't remember what I entered. I know my friend Red—whose fiery hair and pale freckled skin put my strawberry-blonde to shame—wanted us to be The Venable Safari Hunters.

In the end we got to vote between three fangless, principal-approved options, and emerged as the Venable All-Stars. This rebranding called for a celebration. Red's father was a songwriter. The school commissioned him to not only pen a new school song, but also to write an original musical for that spring's play. We learned the words to the anthem and belted it in assembly, high off the sound of our own voices:

We're All-Stars
that's who we are
at Venable School, everyone's an All-Star

The Jefferson School was not always where I believed it to be. It began in a single room, just blocks away near the train station on West Main Street. At the end of the Civil War, an abolitionist and educator named Anna Gardner was sent south by the New England Freedman's Aid Society to open a school for the formerly enslaved. She admired Thomas

Jefferson—whose preserved plantation home looms over the city from a hill a few miles southeast of downtown—and named the school after him. It became a roaming entity for the education of Black children in Charlottesville, expanding with the student population to occupy various larger buildings in the neighborhood over the years, but stopped at grade eight. Black parents seeking a high school education for their children had to send them out of town. In 1924, community members petitioned the city to build a local high school for these underserved students.[1]

When the city gave in and began construction on the building that became the Jefferson School of my youth, they simultaneously constructed a new elementary school for the white children of an adjacent neighborhood. Where the Jefferson High School was factory-ordered and perfunctory, the other building was architected to be Jeffersonian, its staircase up to columns symbolically gesturing toward the ascent the white students would eventually make to Jefferson's University of Virginia, their birthright in the estimation of the local white supremacist backing the project. The school opened in 1925, a year before the Jefferson High School's completion, and was named Venable, after Charles Scott Venable, a deceased UVA math professor, city school board member, and textbook author who had also served as a Confederate Colonel, aide-de-camp to General Robert E. Lee.[2]

In the May 19th, 1934 edition of *The Reflector*, a paper that reported on Black life in Charlottesville during the Jim Crow era, Thomas Jerome Sellers, a journalist who was in the first graduating class at Jefferson High, reviewed a play at his alma mater:

> The Senior Class of Jefferson High School presented a play entitled "No Account David," in the Auditorium last Monday at eight thirty. A large crowd attended and the play was a great success. Three vaudevillians came to the little town just in time to save Grandma Golden's house from the clutches of the mortgager. Between the first and second act Miss Thelma Watson sang "Dusk and the Shadows Falling."[3]

The original musical written for the rebirth of Venable's student population as All-Stars was set in the 1950s. I was not cast as a Venable All-Star. I wasn't even cast as a child; I was cast as the adult male jerk at the local soda shop, the play's main setting. I was overjoyed. For most of elementary school I was enamored with these kinds of jobs. My greatest dream in life—one I'd written out and drawn in a recent assignment—was to be a taxi driver in Virginia Beach. When Mom wondered about my lack of ambition and asked why, my reply was "because I'd get to meet people."

Soda jerk was solid casting. "What'll it be?" I practiced saying. Decked out in my apron and cap, I wiped the counter and watched as the Venable All-Stars came and went, playing out their little dramas of self-discovery. In this service role, as on the playground, I was happy as a go-between, noncommittal, shifting between friend groups.

White kids and Black kids made up the majority of the cast, reflecting the demographics of the school at the time. Venable's central district straddled various neighborhoods in what remained—in the late 80s and early 90s—a segregated Charlottesville. We were more-or-less unaware of this as kids in the classrooms, until the final bell rang and we headed out in different directions to our respective neighborhoods, the white students largely to the north, the Black students largely to the east. The epoch the original musical depicted was the revisionist 50s idyll of *Grease* and *Happy Days*, all aesthetic and no hatred, everyone at school together, no one barred from the soda shop. The antagonists of the Venable All-Stars in this original musical were a gang of students from a rival school: The Blue Meanies. I served everyone sodas and didn't get involved. The rival school tried to start a rumble, and the Venable All-Stars had to sing their theme song to hold the Blue Meanies back, eventually teaching them that everyone, despite their differences, could be embraced as an All-Star. The moral in the end was inclusivity.

In the real 1958, the Virginia legislature voted for Massive Resistance against national school desegregation, and in turn the governor took control of and shut down Venable Elementary, as well as the whites-only city high school, rather than allow them to be racially integrated, making Virginia the first state, and Charlottesville one of the first communities to do so. Venable remained closed for that entire school year. In September of 1959 a federal judge ordered the city schools to re-open, and a group of

Black students entered these previously all-white buildings, three to the high school and nine to Venable. In 2011, these students and their groundbreaking act were commemorated with two identical plaques, one at the high school and the other on the front lawn of Venable Elementary. *Triumph of the Charlottesville 12*, they read.[4]

Civil Rights education was not absent from my Venable education. We learned about the Charlottesville twelve, their triumph framed as a benchmark that solved systemic problems—or at least placed them in the background—in perpetuity. Every February we had extensive curricular and creative Black History Month activities. We wrote poems called *Black is Beautiful* and placed them on the walls beside our gold star charts. Julian Bond, the Black activist, anti-segregation politician, first president of the Southern Poverty Law Center, and UVA professor visited my fourth-grade class to teach us about the Civil Rights Movement. I got his autograph and stored it alongside the autograph I'd gotten from Muhammad Ali and a Vicki Vale trading card, my most precious possessions.

Stars make up a miniscule percentage of the night sky. I learned so much, but at any given moment I was failing to learn astronomically more.

My family is from the deepest south, and the little satellite that Mom and Dad formed in Virginia after their graduate educations at UVA was essentially a Yankee faction in relation to my Alabama ancestry. This ancestry includes the Bankhead political dynasty: three generations of United States legislators that spanned the late 19th and early 20th century. My great-great grandfather was John H. Bankhead II, who during his tenure in the Alabama House of Representatives drafted election laws which included a series of tests and poll taxes designed specifically to disenfranchise newly eligible Black voters, halting the progress of their communities immeasurably.[5] This vile specificity was not talked about in our family, and much of my ancestors were exalted at arm's length, the rose-coloring much more present for my Alabama cousins. One cousin, kept in the dark about anything but the noble achievement of these family men, dressed up as our great-great grandfather John for a fourth grade Alabama history pageant. I imagine he received a gold star for this performance.

In 1964, Jefferson closed as an all-Black elementary school, and shortly reopened as a fully integrated school for sixth graders, completing the city school system's transition out of explicit segregation. The Jefferson School building had long stood next to—and served—the Vinegar Hill neighborhood, established in the 1870s by the formerly enslaved, and built up over the century to become Charlottesville's major Black residential and business community. It occupied a central area between the downtown business district and UVA, and in the 1960s this was seen as prime real estate to white developers and city officials. Urban Renewal—another cover-up of a phrase, like Massive Resistance—was used to justify the city's plans to raze Vinegar Hill, a destruction funded by federal tax dollars. Because of racist voter policies like those enacted by my great-great-grandfather, the Black residents of Vinegar Hill had little say in what was about to happen, and in 1965 the bulldozers rolled through and demolished their homes—homes they owned and cared for, generational properties that their children could have inherited.[6,7] Businesses closed for good or struggled to relocate. Families moved away or were moved into public housing.[8] The area that was once Vinegar Hill stood empty for many years, a grassy desolation, a wound in the heart of Charlottesville. In 1989, when my classmates and I stood at the edge of our Jefferson School playground and looked out across the former neighborhood, all we saw was the sprawl of a parking lot.

If a gold star was a scratch-and-sniff it'd smell like fresh asphalt, paved over something green that was trying to grow.

In the late stages of my time at Venable, I and a handful of others traded in our hordes of gold stars for a label: gifted. For one day each week we'd hop on a second bus and get dropped at off at another city elementary school to join our fellow gifted in a different kind of education marked by creative expression and exploration, a program called Quest. In Quest we were surrounded by the aura that we had some inherent talent rather than opportunity and privilege. The percentage of white students in this gifted oasis was far higher than the percentage of Black students. A new era of internal segregation took root under the guise of achievement. As Questers, our specialness was a cloaked incentive to prevent white flight. A reward for remaining.

Since the early days of integration in Charlottesville, white families with the means (and sometimes bolstered by government tuition vouchers) had gone with the private school option to form their own mini resistances. In my era these alternatives included the country-club-crowd school, where lacrosse was a religion, and the hippy school in the woods, where I attended summer arts camp and saw my first ghost. White families that kept their students in the city school system got their own gold stars in the form of ballooning enrollment in the gifted program, and in the form of redistricting to keep class sizes low and reading scores high, feeding the pipeline of white students from Quest to Advanced Placement to college admission. On the backside of these gold stars were long commutes for Black students to their designated elementary school and a widening achievement gap along racial lines.[9] Students denied the gifted label and all the opportunities that accompanied it found they had little room to escape from the track on which they were placed, once the stars had set.

When I finished fourth grade and prepared to flee Venable for the melodrama of middle school, I left something behind: a self-portrait. Instead of a gold star it got galleried on the wall in the hallway of the highest floor. The day I drew it our teacher had set up small mirrors at our desks. We all studied our own faces and captured them on the canvases in thick pencil. I spent three minutes sketching myself—the jutting jaw and sinking eyes from my hardest year yet—and the remainder of the hour drawing the background:

a horrorscape of gravestones and dead trees, werewolves howling and skeletal hands bursting up from the ground. The day before summer break, I stood in the hall in front of the mounted portrait and admired my sketchy boy and all his sinister surroundings. A teacher walked up next to me and asked, "Where's Waldo?" I pointed and said, "He's walking up to Dracula's castle with a knife in his back."

Development continued to transform West Main Street into the new century, but the Jefferson School building remained a dangling question. The Jefferson Alumni Association and other community activists, educators, and historians began a long campaign to preserve and restore the building.[10] In 2013, after many years of fundraising and construction, the building re-opened as the Jefferson School City Center, a multi-tenant complex for local nonprofits anchored by the new African American Heritage Center. Its mission: "to honor and preserve the rich heritage and legacy of the African-American community of Charlottesville-Albemarle, Virginia and to promote a greater appreciation for, and understanding of, the contributions of African-Americans and peoples of the diaspora locally, nationally and globally."

I grew up and became a teacher. For many years, I taught creative writing to high school students at a University of Virginia summer program, hosted since 2012 at a haunted women's college on a former plantation an hour south of town. In 2018, two local filmmakers visited the program to screen a documentary they'd filmed in the late 1980s and early 1990s, about the changing face of Charlottesville's West Main Street, the sense of loss felt by the elderly residents and merchants who've endured the damage of Urban Renewal.[11] I watched Rebecca McGinness—a student at Jefferson who then taught there for 45 years, from 1915-1960—speak about educating generations of her community's children in the midst of their oppression. She said she felt blessed. Cutaway footage showed the front of Venable, a gaggle of kids bounding out the doors, past the columns and down the wide stairs, All-Stars of my exact tenure there. I half-expected to see myself among them.

The following summer I booked a tour of The Jefferson School African American Heritage Center for my creative writing students. Because the summer program took place out of town, each year there was one field trip day where our group could visit Charlottesville and walk the UVA Grounds. Our tour was scheduled for after lunch. I arrived early at the building, in my own car, while my students rode the free trolley. I parked in the new garage, climbed the stairs past what used to be my playground, and entered the left wing of the building: the African American Heritage Center. Old wooden school desks lined the edge of the long corridor. I could almost smell the perfume. On the wall were black-and-white photographs—taken in 1963 by a county high school student—of daily life in the Vinegar Hill neighborhood. In one frozen image a group of Black schoolchildren cross the street. In the background of another, a man leans back in a chair against the wood-slat wall of his house. In the foreground, a girl jumps rope on the dirt road, smiling. I glanced at the title, a name: "Emma Lewis." I looked into her eyes. I sat down in a desk that could have been mine, thirty years ago, and waited for my students to arrive. Waited to finally learn something.

CONSTELLATION

The glow-in-the-dark night sky stickers were repulsive in the sun, not suited for the light of day. Each five-sided fat star and circular planet was a sicker pale green than even Mr. Yuk. Corpse-colored. We had to charge them with our bedside lamps to coax out the glow, spending anticipatory hours finishing homework or saying our prayers or singing *Buffalo gals won't you come out tonight?* with our tender parents, looking up at the ugly constellation that clashed with the white ceiling paint on which it stuck. We hoped—as we did with the real stars outside—that the beauty would re-emerge each night, on faith alone, like developing photographs used to be, no instant affirmation. Then we'd give them darkness to allow their shine.

When I was five and my younger brother was two, we moved into our true childhood home, the expansive one in the woods near the center of town. We each got our own bedroom, and shortly after, our own glow-in-the-dark night sky sticker set. We divvied up our favorite pieces. My brother liked the shooting stars and comets, I preferred the ringed planets—the Saturns and the Uranuses. We craned our little necks and schemed. There's nothing sadder to a child than a blank ceiling. (As I write this, social media is trying to sell me a light machine that will fill my bedroom with sparkling galaxies.) In our youth these stickers were the pinnacle of cosmic creation, antithetical to the gold stars at school, a private artistic expression, nothing graded. Here, kid: take these stars and make your own sky.

We balled up our sticker trash, now full of galactic gaps, and stuffed the wads in our closets. These closets would accumulate illicit items in their dark out-of-reach corners over the course of our adolescences—lighters and the things they ignite, pictures of tits and dicks—but our ceilings stayed innocent, marred only by their impossible night skies. Our house was built into the side of a hill and our corner bedrooms inhabited the highest points above the basement apartment that our parents rented out to grad students. My brother had his corner and I had mine, different views and different boyhoods. Neither of us were Geminis.

From underneath my stickered ceiling I could see the woods that dropped off steeply to the road below, where teens parked their cars to make out, and where I'd one day get spotlighted by the cops. I could see the architecture professor erect his masterpiece next door, a transparent monolith that he drove women back to in his Porsche. I could see the walnut tree that dropped its harvest like grenades on the roof above my head, and where I'd always wanted to build a treehouse but instead only drew blueprints that my teacher annotated with "This is a fancy treehouse, but how do you get to it?" From underneath my sky I could see the only tall structure in the area, a brick building where Dad went each day—his office on the top floor, its window at equal height with mine—and worked alongside the woman who would soon become my stepmom. From underneath my sky I got out a poster board and paint and wrote "Night is dark and quiet everyone is sleeping. Dark shadows are creeping. Night night night."

From underneath his sky my brother could see our backyard and the pool he was accidentally dropped into as an infant by a loving and forever repentant aunt. He could see the rhododendron blossoms pop in spring, the deer families crossing through in the early mornings, sticking together, gathering in front of the creepy tool shed to chew and watch us all wake up and prepare our lunchboxes and go stand at the end of the street under the dead end sign. He could hear me picking his door lock with a table knife, demanding attention, could see me in the den late at night, banging on our parents' door and crying to be let in, to get help switching off my mind. He could see our parents' bedroom, could see them silently yelling, going for each other's throats more and more every day, could see it become only Mom's room. He could see the pool unused and covered up. Underneath his sky my brother got out a notecard and crayon and wrote "Rain sometimes makes waterfalls."

Our ceilings were out of reach for Mom, and the sprawling, flat house was a must for her, a paraplegic who had used a wheelchair since she was young. She cared for us with her voice, gave direction and caution as I stood on my bed to stick my constellation up. Then I stood on my brother's bed, had him hand me his stickers, helped him realize his vision. He was smaller then, naturally, and he would stay small until I went away to college.

If the glow-in-the-dark night sky was a scratch-and-sniff, it'd smell like a growth spurt.

In middle school I made a friend who had filled her ceiling with glow-and-the-dark stars, an epic expression, its own light source. Another friend told me that she grossly overestimated how many stars she had, and had clustered them all together like a sad spill and then run out, had squandered her cosmos and was confronted from above with mostly inky darkness, the void. The same exact thing happened with mine. My constellation was a little smudge, filling the space above my head and nowhere else, a mutated astrological sign, a unicorn with a knife in its back. This worked fine for me, filled my line of vision with a satisfying glow that soothed me toward dreams, second Uranus to the right and straight on till morning.

My brother's sky covered the perfect amount of ceiling space, and looked like a real constellation. It was better than mine. He was better at everything.

Better at talking, better at collecting stuffed animals, at packing his bed and burying himself in them to sleep. Better at showing affection, better at giving gifts, better at slipping notes under my door for no reason, notes that said, "Dear Henry, I hope you have a happy week and a happy long life." Better at *Super Mario World*, better at *Zombies Ate My Neighbors*, better at yelling at me when I'd hog the controller, better at Donald Duck impressions. Better at painting, better at papier-mâché, better at sketching Mom's wheelchair, better at self-portraits, better at drawing blood. Better at karate, better at taking a punch, better at telling, better at being slammed in closets and locked in the creepy shed, better at throwing a chair through a window, better at breaking out, better at putting up with my shit—my literal shit when I'd make him look at my shit. Better at swimming, better at getting lost at the water park after snorkeling with sharks, better at worrying Mom to death, better at staying in one place until we found him, better at reading. Better at soccer, better at removing ticks, better at breaking his bones, better at coming home from camp early when it got bad, better at healing, better at guitar, better at piano, better at singing in the choir and singing in the shower, better at practicing. Better at improving—at getting better. Better at pushing Mom in her chair, better at pushing people away, better at carving out his space, better at being by himself, better at asking our parents point blank, better at taking their divorce to heart, better at running off, better at holding a grudge, better at holding the cats, better at howling at the moon, better at keeping secrets, better at spending his allowance, better at coming up with Halloween costumes, better at building snowmen, better at navigating the bamboo forest in the neighbor's backyard, better at picking songs on the jukebox at Pizza Hut (not just the same Wilson Phillips ballad every single Friday), better at kicking a hole in the door. Better at eating meat, better at cooking, better at helping Mom in the kitchen, better at feeding himself, at not agonizing over every calorie. Better at shaving his face with the light on so he could see what he was doing, not hiding in the dark from his own reflection and carving his cheeks and chin all bloody. Better at being cute, better at being straight, better at skateboarding, better at showing off, better at not caring, better at becoming a young man, better at petitioning the city to decrease light pollution so people could see the real stars, better at dyeing his hair, better at leaving. Better in cities, better at adapting, better at staying away from Charlottesville. Better at going out, better at making friends, better at playing shows, better at travelling the world, better at being on TV, better at drinking, better at drugs, better at forgetting, better at rock bottom, better at getting help, better at recovery, better at sobriety. Better at finding home, better at meeting people where they are, better at continuing to grow, better at caring, better at living in the moment, better at nursing his wounds, better at driving all night, better at speeding up, better at slowing down, better at remembering to breathe, better at knowing when to stop.

The only thing I'm better at is writing all this out. The least impressive skill.

CHIQUITA

The best meal I ever ate was a Chiquita banana. Its taste was superior to everything I'd eaten before and everything I've eaten since, because I ate it minutes after almost dying. The flavor was as precious as my little life.

My near-death started because of the environment. I'd learned about the environment in school the previous spring, and it was such a big deal I filled a page of my diary with "I learnd about the ENViORNMent," the *o* a poorly rendered globe. This environment was epic and nonspecific. In the 90s of my childhood, conservationist signifiers like Earth Day and recycling were self-satisfied edifices: awareness of them was all that mattered, the whole ball game. As a performance of my awareness, I wore a shirt of a rainbow globe, its vivid colors not far from Lisa Frank, each ecosystem teeming with dolphins and birds and all kinds of flora. I adored the shirt and dared to wear it to sports camp.

The University of Virginia sports camp took place in different rec centers scattered around Grounds, emptied of students for the summer. That day we were in the gym to play water polo. Locker rooms were never a friendly place for me, but as I dried myself off things got even more hostile. "Hey smart-ass," some tough kid said. I was still branded from the summer's first roll call, when mine was the last name Coach read, and he met my eyes through process of elimination. "Who else could I be?" I had said, and he'd replied, "you could be a smart-ass who I don't like." His words were now seared onto the steak of insecurity beating inside my chest. Smart-ass stuck as my new name. The tough kid and his cronies surrounded me, snatched my environment shirt and threw it on top of the row of tall steel lockers. Laughing, they left me alone with my out-of-reach shirt. Free of anyone's eyes, I decided to get a running start from across the room, leap up and rescue the environment.

It worked—the shirt was in my hand—but as I fell backwards my other hand caught the locker edge and pulled the enormous row down on top of me. The steel scraped diagonally across my chest and my back hit the soggy floor. The row of lockers, which could have easily crushed my body completely, stopped a centimeter from my face: the small wooden bench behind me had halted the lockers' fall. I crawled out from underneath, clutched my environment shirt and surveyed the scene. If this little slab of wood had been a few inches further to the right I knew I'd be dead. I imagined myself out-of-body, viewing the site of my death on my way to whatever came next.

If the afterlife was a scratch-and-sniff it'd smell like chlorine.

Minutes later, I sat in the passenger seat of Mom's car and she handed me the Chiquita banana. Before peeling the banana, I peeled the blue Chiquita sticker off and pressed it to the back of my hand. This was unnecessary—you don't have to take a sticker off of a banana like you do with an apple—but it was fun, a bonus. That day, the sticker removal was a ritual. Placing it on the back of my hand marked my survival. I clutched the arm of Mom's wheelchair, folded and wedged behind our seats. After my brush with annihilation, I felt closer to Mom than ever before. Maybe that was *my* near-death, I thought, maybe we're more alike now. Mom's near-death was out in the open for everyone to see, always.

Mom hummed the jingle from the Chiquita banana commercials of her youth. The sticker that now decorated the back of my hand was a blue oval with a yellow ring, the white word Chiquita in the middle. Above the word was a yellow woman with one hand resting on her hip and one hand held in the air, an implied shimmy. She had flowery sleeves and a fruit headdress, a facsimile of Carmen Miranda, the Portuguese-Brazilian performance icon. This image of a real woman had recently replaced the previous mascot, an anthropomorphic Banana with the same style who starred in gleeful colonialist commercials.[1] Mom's singing voice filled the car as we drove home. I knew she had a deep connection with the Chiquita brand. When my brother was a baby, Mom handmade a banana costume for him to wear, the hood a fleecy yellow extension of his curly blonde hair, a black stem on top. In the center she sewed her take on the iconic blue sticker, no banana woman or real woman, just the embroidered word *Chiquita*.

If the Chiquita sticker was a scratch-and-sniff, you'd think it'd smell like banana.

As I consumed the holy fruit on my near-death day, I looked down and Mom and I both noticed the blood, seeping from my chest gash and staining the rainbow globe. I pulled up my shirt and showed her. She handed me a napkin. I told her about my accident with the row of lockers, fear and relief welling up from inside my heart, that quiet organ that almost wasn't. "You're lucky," Mom said, "you don't need stitches, it'll just be a scab."

This chapter could have been called Scab instead. This book is morbid and that's something you'll have to get used to. These stories aren't heading anywhere good. Neither is my town, or this country, or this environment. Scabs are nature's stickers, sent from heaven to stop our bleeding. What's underneath them is usually gory.

I didn't tell Mom about the volley of names I'd been called during my day at sports camp, didn't tell her why I was in the locker room last and alone. The tough kids of the 60s gave Mom a shitty nickname, too: Scab-Eater. This was an original wound for her. One day she had a scab, and picked it. The tough kids dared her to eat it. She ate it, to prove she was tough. But it was a set-up. She was Scab-Eater. I was Son of Scab-Eater.

Chiquita is what you call a little girl, or someone you want to make feel like a little girl. "What an adorable little girl," a woman in a checkout line once said about me. I can't remember if Mom corrected her. I was rosy with a lot of hair. Sometimes I think I was Mom's daughter. The first born, feminine, a reflection of her. "Don't pick your scabs," she'd say, "don't eat your scabs." When Dad left, it hit me just how much I wasn't man-of-the-house material. I was glad to have a brother; he could be the son.

Mom called me Mabel in public all the time. It was shorthand for the old charm school rhyme, reminding me about table manners:

Mabel Mabel, strong and able
Get your elbows off the table

I'm all elbows. We'd be sitting in a crowded restaurant and she'd snap "Mabel" to reprimand me. People at other tables might have thought my name was Mabel. I liked this. Mabel became the main character of the stories I'd write in school. A supernatural girl, a rip-off of Roald Dahl's Matilda. As a teen I'd pretend to be Mabel in AOL sex chat rooms—the fucked, not the fucker. Mabel was always somewhere inside, waiting to be called out.

When I'd come home from other locker rooms, where boys put me in sleeper holds and said I was built like their grandfather, and stand destroyed by her bed, Mom would ask me if I thought I might be gay. This was a tremendous generosity, but I didn't know how to answer. The only place I'd heard "queer" was in the hybrid dodgeball game we played at school, "Smear the Queer." The queer wasn't something desirable to be, but we all took turns being it, being a target. I didn't have the words to describe my attractions yet, to make them make sense.

My long-deceased cousin Tallulah was a famous bisexual. She was an actress and socialite in New York and Hollywood and London and dated many well-known women, referring to herself proudly as "ambisextrous."[2] But I didn't learn about her sex life until adulthood; this wasn't the aspect of her that was discussed in my house. To us she was The Black Widow in the *Batman* TV series and the model for Cruella de Vil. Her booming voice and caustic personality were a fond family resemblance, a chapter now closed. Her caricature graced the wall of our den—a cartoon lady lounging on a chaise—framed above a portrait of my brother and me and Mom and Dad, our dissolving foursome.

I thought about dressing as Tallulah for Halloween, tapping into her spirit, but I knew no one would have a clue who I was. I went as a witch instead. A pumpkin. A mummy. Mom handmade the costumes to wear alongside my banana brother. In her bathroom she wrapped me head-to-toe in toilet paper and masking tape, painted my face, bloodied my lips and eyes, prepared me to enter the night.

The day after my near-death, I stood topless and looked at my wound in the mirror. One scab had formed at the bottom part of the long crevice, a reminder that I had almost died. Today almost wasn't. I fingered the scab to see if it was ripe for removal.

A scab is a scratch-and-sniff. It smells like bonding.

I chose not to peel. I chose to wait. To grow away from death for a while.

REINFORCER

The reinforcer is an anomaly: a sticker with a practical application. It's not meant to signal anything, to warn or exclaim. The small white donut sticks over a ripped ring in notebook paper, allowing the paper to remain firm in its binder, prolonging its use. The adhesive nature of the reinforcer is the totality of its value. For this reason, it can be found in the store's boring aisles—the school supplies, or, god forbid, the office supplies—far from the fun zone.

Reinforcers have no personality. They were a good match for me. My favorite color was white. My favorite chewy candies were the white ones, like the great white shark in the aquatic fruit snacks or the Airheads called "White Mystery"—a sugary blank slate that upon tasting could magically end up being any of the other varieties. I loved the cognitive dissonance of tasting strawberry with no pink in sight. Flavorless flavor. I placed a reinforcer on the tip of my stuck-out tongue.

If a reinforcer was a scratch-and-sniff it'd smell undying.

From a pack of hundreds, I'd maybe use one reinforcer a year for its intended purpose. The remaining white donuts were recreational. I found pleasure in peeling them off their base, pleasure in covering every inch of my notebook with them, their circular blandness overflowing, becoming a pox.

My classmates showed off their sticker collections—scrapbooks where every page was stuck with a new set of expressions, a new performance of self. I wasted my energy with reinforcers. I had so many to dot my notebooks and my body with, I peeled them constantly and was nowhere near the end. A cover-up, their blizzard formed a spiraling white tundra unto itself. A new surface for sticking.

Mom cast a spell in her diary, wrote that she believed I'd escaped the chicken pox that had just loosened their ferocious grip on my brother. I must have had them as a baby, "a benign case," she wrote and hoped. A week later the pox came for me. I had just experienced my first kiss, in our back yard with the niece of a neighbor. The sudden red spots that peppered my skin felt like a consequence. I was happy to miss middle school. The ribbed blue couch in our den became my home. Mom went off to work and I had total quiet in which to enjoy my itching pain. I discovered that we had MTV. I discovered I was a loser baby so why don't you kill me. My school supplies sat unused for a week, atrophied, until Mom made me work on my make-up assignments, dropped off by an older boy. I stuck the reinforcers to my fingers, to the TV remote.

The pox hit their peak on the weekend, when it was time for visitation with Dad, as designated by the separation agreement. He had recently moved to a cozy A-frame house in the woods behind a pre-school, an ideal weekend retreat. Inside was a painting by a local artist that didn't hang but instead stayed propped in a corner near the bathroom where I took long oatmeal baths to curb the itching. The painting showed two faces side-by-side: on the left a freckly regular kid, his hair sticking up and his buck teeth showing, and on the right a smudged red-faced monster kid, turned inside-out. Regular kid was labelled *Sam* and monster kid was labelled *Steve*. The pox gave my brother bad spots, but he maintained the appearance of a boy. I became haggard, my face disfigured. I looked in the mirror and scared myself, unrecognizable. Reflective surfaces became my enemy. I'd transformed from Sam into Steve and didn't think I could ever go back. The pox would stay with me. I turned my head away and wept and read and made long phone calls to the older boy about the band we were going to start, sang him my epic songs. He asked me why they didn't have any choruses.

In my ugliness the reinforcers became cosmetic. I'd stick them over every disgusting bump, covering my cheeks and neck and shoulders with even whiter white, until I felt effaced. I shuffled around, an exiled creature in Dad's weird house, far from a civilization that would reject me.

This was the experience that truly made me a writer. Not because I got any writing done, but because I learned to bask in being alone. The isolation would become my life as an author. The infinite not-writing, the constant pajamas. The self-loathing. When I emerged from my hideous chrysalis, I wrote my first play.

This is the book's introduction. Like most things in life, it's arriving late. Stickers can be excuses.

You're experiencing my second chance. A memoir in 20 stickers, randomly arranged and full of contradictions. An attempt to make my identity a little more tangible. Your chosen set of stickers would be different, like your desires. If you really care about the history of adhesive labels, just go on the internet. Stickers are a means to an end.

Charlottesville always seemed to me like a vortex for stickers—their chaos littering bar windows and lampposts and cars and the gates that rose to allow entry into parking lots. In whatever arrangement, stuck by however many hands, they created cognitive whiplash, never adding up. *Coexist* coexisted with band names and brand logos and authoritative statements. Maybe this is true of every small city, every college town. I don't know. I wasn't raised anywhere else.

PROUD PARENT

Fred has always been a member of my family. Fred was with my mother long before I was born, and Fred lived with my mother before and after my father left the house for good. Fred bumps against my bedroom door every morning to wake me. Whenever I leave the house, Fred enters my room to scavenge for drugs or dirty dishes. Fred is never far from my mother. Fred sits and watches her in bed and on the toilet and in the tub. In order to escape Fred, my mother has to be thrown into a pool or lake where Fred can't follow.

The creator of the "Proud Parent of an Honor Roll Student" bumper sticker was probably the proud parent of an honor roll student. The creator of the "My Kid Can Beat Up Your Honor Roll Student" bumper sticker was probably not the parent of an honor roll student, but they were still proud. Proud of the beating.

There have been many versions of Fred, sometimes two at a time. Only my mother keeps count. But Fred is always their name, and no one knows why. Fred is in all my childhood drawings of my mother, and thanks to Fred all our tables are missing a chair. Fred catches the light. When I took my mother's picture for a dating site, she asked me to crop Fred out. She says Fred is the reason she's still alone.

A bumper sticker is an extension of the car. Proud Parents who sticker their bumpers see their children as extensions of themselves. *My Honor Roll Sticker Affirms My Good Parenting.* My mother has another extension. A co-parent.

There's a picture of Fred at the end of a hallway in my mother's house. In it my mother and I have colorful swirls painted on our faces, and I'm holding her shoulders and Fred is between us.

If a proud parent bumper sticker was a scratch-and-sniff it'd smell like exhaustion.

I pushed Fred around so much I dream about endless ramps. My mother pushed Fred around so much she got carpal tunnel. Children look at Fred funny and their parents squint down at my mother. Fred makes maître d's nervous and allows us to skip lines at amusement parks. I have to keep Fred out of sight when flagging taxis because if the drivers see Fred they won't stop. Fred comes into psychiatrist's offices with my mother and me, and pulls my mother out angrily at the first sign of blame. Fred runs over my toes, and it's my fault for being in the way.

The sticker becomes a vehicle for a parent's projection. *My Kid Will Exceed Expectations. My Kid Will Carry Me in My Old Age.* Fred is where I project.

Fred used to ride along with us in the low car, folded and wedged behind the driver's seat, or sometimes stuffed in the trunk. Now my mother doesn't always detach. She steers

Fred onto a hydraulic lift that pulls them up into the SUV intact. The door swallows them both and drops them at the steering wheel.

Two surfaces to sticker: Fred's back and the SUV's bumper. One inside the other. Two spaces for pride.

My Kid Told Me I Was Probably His Best Friend and That I was Beautiful and Funny and Smart and I'm in a Wheelchair and That Makes Me Special

A sheer headwind precedes a benign summer rain and cuts a gash across our town, toppling forests at their roots and scattering piles of branches into windows and cars and opening the tops of newly renovated houses to the sky. The power goes out and I see horizontal water pellets, and I pluck up my mother from her wheelchair and rush her down to the basement. By the time I'm cradling her at the bottom of the stairs, the storm has ended, and she demands I return her to Fred.

Resting on a high table in our living room is a framed black-and-white photo of my mother as a young woman. She sits with a broad smile and wears a sash that reads Miss Wheelchair Alabama. Behind the photo there are flat black cutouts of birds pasted to the window, so the real ones don't smack into it and kill themselves.

I can hear Fred coming on hardwood or carpet, just unquiet enough, but these early warnings aren't important. Fred is always approaching. On my mother's command to fill tires with air, I kneel for Fred. Fred shows me the inaccessible world, even in my earliest memories, when wheels tower above. I learn to count on the spokes. Metal not-fingers.

My Honor Rolls

When I was ten years old, my mother left me alone with Fred, so we joined forces. My mother's legs would shake involuntarily when she sat in Fred, but I willed mine to be still. I transferred to Fred from the sofa, dragging my feet along with me, and we rolled around the house. I used a grabber to reach cookies from a high shelf, popped wheelies over doorjambs, and then I went outside to check the mail. At the top of our driveway, I lost control of Fred, careening and gathering speed down the street. Fred's wheels burned my hands when I tried to stop, but I wouldn't move my legs and I wouldn't leap out to save myself. Fred and I were committed to this experience.

I have two tiny parallel scars, like tire tracks, below my lips.

PARENTAL ADVISORY
EXPLICIT CONTENT

I became an orphan on a snow day.

I knew it was a snow day before getting out of bed and looking out the window because Mom hadn't knocked. Every school day she'd roll up to my brother and my doors and knock and gently call out shortened versions of our names, and then, "Up and at 'em." That day there was just thick quiet. The light was different. I could sense the snow. I opened my blinds and saw it still falling. I took a long shower, got dressed, and found Mom at the breakfast table. "Two-hour delay," she said. "I thought I'd let you sleep."

A two-hour delay was to see if the snow would let up so the bus could come get me and take me to my school across town. It was worse than no snow day at all. I ate and prayed for the blizzard to continue. It did. When I got back to my room and turned on the boombox the DJ said, "Charlottesville City: cancelled." I clicked him off and grabbed a random cassette. A black tape that just said "PRINCE" in Dad's handwritten sharpie. I turned it up loud enough to wake my brother through the wall. Later in life, I'll listen to Prince sing more than I've listened to any of my loved ones talk, but on the snowy morning he was a curiosity, an icon from an earlier time, from *Batman*. This cassette was a curiosity too, a relic in a small box of cassettes left behind by a leaving Dad. The song was about creaming and getting on top.

The story goes that Karenna Gore—eldest daughter of then-Senator Al Gore and his wife Tipper—had a day in the mid-80s like I was having in the mid-90s. A Prince-listening day. She'd been gifted the hugely popular album Purple Rain and was playing it in earshot of her mother. When they reached the fifth track Darling Nikki (my favorite), Mother Gore was appalled by Prince's explicit stanza:

> *I knew a girl named Nikki*
> *I guess you could say she was a sex fiend*
> *I met her in a hotel lobby*
> *masturbating with a magazine*

In reaction, alongside other powerful DC wives who'd had similar shocking experiences with mainstream music and their children's impressionable ears, she formed the Parents Music Resource Center (PMRC). This non-profit watchdog group sent fundraising letters to a network of influential parents, and lobbied for music companies to impose warning and rating systems on albums, as the Motion Picture Association of America had on films since the 1960s. In the resulting Senate hearing, Gore suggested that instead of a rating system, the companies could voluntarily label their product. On November 1st, 1985, a sticker was born.[1]

Created by the Recording Industry Association of America, the *Parental Advisory Explicit Lyrics* sticker was a masterpiece of magnetism. Stuck uniformly to the lower-right corner—the *Parental* and *Explicit Lyrics* in white letters against black, sandwiching the *Advisory* in taller black letters against white; this label invigorated even the blandest of album covers. The promised vulgarity sparked the imagination of every transgressive kid on Earth and drew them to the dirtiest shit on the shelves. An undeniable backfire, like most censorship.

My parents wouldn't buy me albums that held the label. Sometimes I tried to slyly scratch the sticker off before bringing it to the checkout, but this proved futile, too much protective plastic or too much tell-tale residue. Dad owned one tape with the sticker, but when he played it around me, he'd skip to only the clean songs. I had a contraband copy of *Appetite for Destruction*, because the sticker was on its outer cellophane wrapper, long tossed by a neighbor who'd bought it and handed it down to me. The lack of sticker wasn't fooling anyone. The guitar riff in "My Michelle" alone is the most obscene thing ever recorded.

The Parental Advisory Explicit Lyrics sticker's natural habitat was the room of my richer friend, because he had his own money to buy music and he had lots of his own space: an attic room like a turret at the top of a castle. His privacy made him a different kind of prince, his name the same as his father's. In his high point of the house where the parents rarely climbed—rarely advised—the black-and-white stickers were everywhere, bold and unashamed. We could play them loud, these songs about killing cops and fucking cops, while we waited three hours for the computer to load an image of two women lying on their stomachs, unclothed and kissing.

On the eighth grade snow day, one hour before I was orphaned, I had thirty dollars in Christmas money and knew exactly how I planned to spend it. This money was tithe for The Antichrist. My school friends had told me I needed to buy his new album. I'd recently done a big clique switch and joined the goths, had gone from drowning in an oversize Weezer T-shirt to drowning in an oversize White Zombie T-shirt. This was the second time I'd walked away from one established friend group to fall in with a marginal one. The first time was in fourth grade, when—on the shredded-rubber playground at Venable—my sporty-boy friends invented a violent game with the special-needs students called "Retard Ram." I told one special-needs student that the sporty boys had said "yr mama," and walked away without seeing the fight that ensued, walked toward the fence on the playground's edge where the geeks hung out, kicking around the green monkey brains—Osage oranges that dropped from shrubs with a thud. The geeks became my new crew for the year. The goths of 8th grade, all five of them, also inhabited the literal outskirts of recess, the end of the long driveway near another fence where they could smoke and skate undisturbed. None of them had the Christmas money for The Antichrist. I was tasked with buying his CD and sharing it. A snow day seemed like a good opportunity. The cold gave me confidence.

I needed a wingman. I called Sled. Sled was my neighbor and he was a year older. He transcended cliques and had already left the city milieu for a private high school. We spent most of our childhood snow days sliding down the hill in front of his house on a metal disk. Indoors, Sled was a nerd lord. He made HyperCard video games and showed me all the *Star Trek* movies. A tastemaker. One time he sat down on our school bus and barfed all over the seat in front of him, and after taking it in, all he said was, "Gross," like a goddamn champ. He probably despised The Antichrist, but it didn't matter. His house was on the way to the strip mall down the hill, and I bundled up and collected him. We weren't at the age for sledding anymore, too old to explore the wooded hills separating our streets, too old to wade in the filthy creek below that held the runoff from a gas station. The record shop was our new magnet. Commerce wouldn't be snowed out, we hoped.

The chain record shop was in the strip mall's best island, the one with the Baskin-Robbins and the Ruby Tuesday where Dad had taken me on Wednesdays to eat bottomless salad bar in that liminal space before his remarriage. We entered the record shop and I beelined for the trough that held The Antichrist. His pale veiny face filled the right half of the CD case. He had long black hair and white makeup and had achieved fame with a spooky pop-metal cover of a song by Annie Lennox; Annie, my idol since always. The Antichrist's advisory wasn't even a sticker anymore, it was printed on the sleeve. It said "Explicit Content"—a measure beyond "Explicit Lyrics" that became the standardized label in 1996. Who knew what horrors lurked inside?

If the Parental Advisory Explicit Content sticker was a scratch-and-sniff it'd smell like a gas leak.

We approached the counter and I placed the CD down, blasé. "Do your parents know you're buying this?" asked the bored clerk. I looked him square in the eyes and answered, "My parents are dead." His boredom evaporated. He looked at Sled. Sled said nothing, but his stoic eyes were confirmation enough of my tragic circumstances. The clerk took my money and I took the album.

Outside, the snow had stopped falling. I stuffed the CD in my coat and we trudged the half-mile back to Sled's house with the quickness of having gotten away with something. When we arrived in his bedroom the CD was no longer in my coat. I searched every part of my clothes and found it nowhere, as if divine intervention had made it disappear. We coated back up and retraced our steps. After a block I saw a square-shaped indentation in the snow by the road. The CD had slipped out. I picked it up and secured it better.

This spot by the tree where I'd dropped The Antichrist will become sacred. In warmer months I'll rollerblade here to smoke cloves, to look up the hill at my bedroom and squint to see if I can make out the ceiling stars. I'll cough. It's not the lyrics that are a danger, it's the lifestyle. I'll bury a pack of cigarettes by a tree, and many years later I'll stay with Mom after her cancer surgery and take a walk and try to excavate them but find only poison ivy. In other countries cigarette packs have a sticker on them: "Smoking Kills." A cancer warning. But everything could have a sticker on it that says "May Cause Cancer." They should just slap one on our birth certificates.

If the cancer sticker was a scratch-and-sniff it'd smell like the thin line of cinnamon you place in the windowsill to keep ants from entering.

As expected, Sled didn't like the album when we finally cued it up on his stereo. As expected, the lyrics were explicit. The opening track's chorus was two words: "fuck it." I was more interested in the promised content, and unfolded the liner notes to indulge my eyes. An out-of-focus Antichrist stood wearing ripped pantyhose and little else, his cock covered with a cast, surgical tubes leading from the tip to masks on the mouths of his bandmates. My eyes widened, as promised. The music took a backseat to the album object and its power.

As I write this, several women have come forward on social media to accuse The Antichrist—whose real name is Brian— of torture, grooming, and sexual assault. For years before, he openly boasted about abusing both strangers and intimate partners, but was shielded from consequence by the binary that moral outrage creates: to oppose The Antichrist was to take the side of the censors, the evangelical oppressors.[2] The vulnerable fans who found comfort in performances of danger and self-destruction were then preyed on in that supposed haven. This predatory pattern, modeled by so many pop star men of the past, is an inseparable element of the music industry.

The iconography of transgression—embodied by the parental advisory—can enable both lyrical and literal violence against women, stickered over and celebrated. I held an admission ticket to this insidious circus in my middle school hands.

The next day, the girl who led the goths grabbed the CD off me and said she'd return it soon, after she'd copied it to cassette. My night went by without withdrawal. During the following lunch, the goth leader said she'd left the CD on my math class desk, but when I got there, the desk was empty. I sat down, confused, and felt the eyes of Mrs. God on me. Mrs. God was our young algebra teacher. She rode a motorcycle and wore a shiny crucifix around her neck. The goths hated her and her born-again bullshit. The joke went, "What's the difference between Mrs. God and a whore in a bag? The bag." I liked her, as I liked all teachers who were disappointed in me, because I was disappointed in myself. The look on her face told me that she had seen the abomination on my desk and confiscated it. Now she stood between me and The Antichrist.

For a fourth-grade assignment I wrote, "When I grow up, I want to go to law school so I can study law like my mother." Mom used her law degree to become something better than a lawyer; she became a professional disability coordinator, working to uphold the Americans with Disabilities Act and ensure accessibility, first with the city, then at the law school, then at the UVA Office For Equal Opportunity and Civil Rights. She was my hero. She was also my mother. We were a diary pair, scribbling away in our separate corners of the house—me writing terse things from my days, like, "Saw

Cool Runnings," or, "My life is a shambles," her archiving all my adorable kid-isms. Mom's diary was addressed to me. She wrote it for an audience, with the intent to some day pass it on, like I'm writing this book to you. My 8th grade diary—chronicling my descent into a world of all black—was not meant for an audience, but Mom read it anyway. I'd left it in her reach and she confronted me, troubled by a line that referred to my new clique as "lovable drug addicts." I told her that this evidence was inadmissible, because she'd acquired it in an unlawful search and seizure.

Before algebra could start, I grabbed my student manual, stood up and approached Mrs. God, channeling Mom's lawfulness as I asked her to point out where in the rulebook it said I couldn't have a CD at school. "I didn't take it 'cuz it's a CD," said Mrs. God, "I took it 'cuz it's satanic." She pronounced it *say*-tanic. I couldn't argue with that. I said a private goodbye to my explicit content.

Months later, Mom came to meet me after school. We'd been called to the office of the assistant principle. Mom was nervous until they told her I was receiving an award for some kind of academic excellence. There was a medal involved, heavy and brass and affixed to a ribbon. Mom and the assistant principle were collectively thrilled with me, showering me with compliments in the cramped office. I tuned them out and stared at my corduroys and thought about how hot I was going to be in black clothes at the amusement park that weekend. When the meeting wrapped up and small talk resumed, the assistant principle said, "We're so grateful to have students like Henry right now. You should have seen the awful thing that was brought to the office—have you heard of this guy?" She proceeded to describe The Antichrist's CD in detail, hinting at the explicit content with equal parts repulsion and fascination. After a long pause, I said, "That's mine."

Mom, unfazed, said, "Can he have it back?"

Clutching The Antichrist and the achievement medal together in my fist, I pushed Mom back to our car and helped her into the driver's seat. I was glad she was alive. She asked if I wanted to play the CD. I took it out of its case, turned it over to look at my reflection, and said, "No." Externalizing my gothness was missing the point.

ROTUNDA

At the beginning of my childhood, Thomas Jefferson was a severed head.

It sat on top of the piano in our living room. Its smooth dead eyes watched me practice. Hard dog-like hair, sharp jaw cocked with confidence. Bust was a word that made kids giggle. This object seemed more aggressive. Like a murder weapon in waiting.

I'd seen it downtown too, a few blocks from the brick church where I went on Tuesdays for piano lessons and the stone church where I went on Sundays to be bored out of my mind. A life-sized silhouette of a working man in a baseball cap held up the unmistakable Jefferson head shape, as if the man had freshly ripped it from Thomas's torso. To most people, the man was simply carrying a bust; I saw decapitation. These silhouettes were muted public art pieces that dotted the downtown pedestrian mall. A block east of the one with Jefferson's head was another silhouette: a child my size held onto with one hand by his mother, her other hand raised in the air, open-palmed. Most people saw this image and saw a woman waving as she tried to control her rowdy child, the obvious intention of the artist. I failed the Rorschach test: what I saw was a mother about to slap her child.

The Downtown Mall is marketed as the bastion of Charlottesville charm, separate from the University. It was created in 1976 when the city closed off eight blocks of a metropolitan street to traffic. Coated with red brick and lined with an ever-developing set of shops, restaurants, and theaters, the Mall set an example for other small Virginia cities to follow, with varying degrees of success. A 1986 article from a neighboring town's local paper notes the Mall's thriving decade in contrast to some other town's failed pedestrian street project, praising how well the Mall "transformed a dying downtown."[1] The hotel at the Mall's west end was built on the ridge at the top of the wasteland that was once Vinegar Hill. A plaque against the short perimeter wall reads, "Vinegar Hill: A Forgotten Neighborhood." In the 90s Vinegar Hill was the name of the indie movie theater on that same ridge, where my buddy Sled worked the box office and handed out popcorn and Italian soda. The red brick the city chose mirrored Jefferson's tastes, paying tribute to the local deity, demonstrating a commitment to collective amnesia. Forgetting is a process. Charm can lay cover.

When you ride the glass elevator near the waving/slapping mother silhouette to the top of the downtown parking garage, Jefferson's Monticello estate comes into view on a nearby hilltop; his house overlooking his university and its surrounding town. He might be disembodied, but in the waning sun he casts a shadow over us all, his brick-laying vision still metastasizing across Monacan indigenous lands. On a nearby traffic island is a statue of Lewis and Clark—Jefferson's errand boys for expanding American genocide—upright and proud, as Sacagawea crouches behind them.

Jefferson's severed head silhouette stands a few feet away from the 4th Street crossing. When I was small it wasn't commonly referred to as 4th Street, because it was just two dead ends—they hadn't taken down the bollards and made this portion of the mall crossable by cars yet.

In the middle of my childhood, Thomas Jefferson was a sticker. His Rotunda: a sparse arrangement of shapes—rounded dome, rectangular columns—that approximated the crown jewel of Jefferson's University of Virginia, his architectural legacy, completed shortly after his death.

As a sticker, the Rotunda was a simple stand-in that announced someone's allegiance, an identifying mark for UVA affiliates: students, alumni, faculty, people like my parents. The sticker shone out from car bumpers on the road that ran from the dead-end house where I was a baby to the steps of the building itself. As a tween, I went to UVA Grounds constantly: to hear string quartets, to visit my parents' offices, to watch college students in the flesh, imagining I might one day become them. The real Rotunda boasted a sunlit central room with no corners. You could stand on one side of the circle and whisper into the wall, and someone else could stand on the opposite side and lean against the wall and hear you loud and clear. More slippery charm, like the serpentine walls that flanked the Rotunda's lawn, hiding the enslaved laborers in the gardens from view; nothing square for Jefferson.

Monticello was architecturally similar to UVA; one could mistake the Rotunda sticker for Jefferson's home instead. I only travelled up the hill to Monticello under duress. The one trip I remember was with my friend Eyeshadow, whose lids had that permanent dark rim that made them bulge out of his face. We went because Dr. Fired told us that's where they sold carnivorous plants.

Dr. Fired was the greatest science teacher in the universe. He invigorated every class with completely unhinged lessons, like making all of us chew a slice of bread for a full hour without swallowing, to note the way our saliva broke down the molecules. (Multiple students puked.) Dr. Fired only lasted one year in the public school system. But in that year, we wanted nothing more than to please him by feeding windowsill bugs to Venus flytraps. Once their fringed green mouth closed over the insect, a slow dissolving process began. The only nearby place to buy these disappointing killers was a stand at Jefferson's Monticello. Eyeshadow and I felt obligated to take the tour. In that era a guide would gesture quickly out the window to the enslaved people's cabin and then draw our attention to some cool shit the master invented with all his spare time.

Over his lifetime Jefferson personally kept over 600 people in bondage, and from America's founding until 1865, Virginia enslaved more people than any other state. UVA's land was cleared by enslaved laborers, and the University scoured the state to rent them—numbering roughly 5,000 over the years—to construct and maintain their Academical Village. When Jefferson died in 1826, months before the Rotunda was completed, professors at UVA purchased enslaved people from his estate. Jefferson's architecture haunts the city of Charlottesville, the moldings and porticos a distraction from the generations of Black lives tortured and destroyed in their creation. The columns uphold this white power. Eyeshadow and I stood on the brick paths we grew out of, predatory plants.

If the Rotunda was a scratch-and-sniff, it would reek.

In 2020, as a reckoning with its violent history, UVA unveiled a Memorial to Enslaved Laborers: a curved wall of names of those whose identities were known, and blank gashes for all those left out of the records. In the center, a timeline of the University's complicity and involvement in slavery, ringing a patch of grass. A sequence of steps leads away in the direction of the north star.[2] Etched into the back of the wall are the eyes of Isabella Gibbons, who was enslaved in a professor's household until emancipation, and later became a teacher at the Jefferson School.[3] The monument has the same circumference as the Rotunda's dome, takes up the same amount of space on the ground, a contrasting footprint.

At the end of my childhood, I became Thomas Jefferson for ten minutes.

It started when The Vampire called me a religious slut, while she chewed my neck to ribbons in the dark playground across the street from the old stone church. We'd grown tired of our usual laps up and down the mall. We crept away through the park, past the drug dealers and the statue of Robert E. Lee, and planted ourselves on a plastic slide where I read her my terrible poetry and she did what vampires do. I was a religious slut because I told her I attended so many different Charlottesville churches, testing out new faiths and new friends. My church at the time was the Presbyterian near the heart of UVA Grounds, next to the small bridge where it was legal to graffiti. "You should join my youth group. We need more boys," The Vampire cooed as she finished her meal. I wore the hickeys proudly to the Ska Against Racism concert the next night, and although Mom helped me apply makeup to cover my shredded neck for school on Monday, I was marked.

The Vampire's youth group was at the Thomas Jefferson Memorial Church, a Unitarian-Universalist enclave just up the street from my Presbyterian, the same street that ended at the steps of the Rotunda, at the feet of the statue of Jefferson, the man to whom all roads lead. The church's naming drew from Jefferson's belief in religious freedom, and this was a vibrant and welcoming interfaith place for a slut like me. As a Presbyterian I sat with my knees together on a stiff couch and discussed sacrifice, or listened as a hyper-Christian kid told me "nobody likes you" in the middle of a ski lift. As Unitarians we formed a cuddle puddle to talk frankly about orgasms, or lay down sleeping bags in a huge circle—a make-out mandala—crickets chirping as our fingers and lips magnetized.

The lock-in was the real rite of passage, an entire night to inhabit the sanctuary and create our own youthful utopia. The girls in the group—which on that night was everyone but me—had a running bit about how they all wanted to fuck Thomas Jefferson, about how hot he was. It was decided that I would play him in our groggy 2AM self-run religious service. I couldn't argue. My hair was slightly red, I had a penis, I was kind of a piece of shit.

The lights dimmed and the ritual began. We lit candles and the girls read invocations from their favorite books. One of the twins grabbed a CD player and queued up "Both Hands," and hearing that song for the first time in that amniotic space, overwhelmed with sleep deprivation and uncontrollable youth, was the only thing in my life that I'd call an epiphany. I wiped the water from my eyes and knew it was almost my moment to become the man whose name was on the building. I had to step outside to fill my lungs. Propping the side door open with a copy of *The Fountainhead* that the other twin had just given me and insisted I read, I lit a bidi, smoked it and mapped the short distance between me and the Rotunda in my mind. A stone's throw to my left was the dead end sign of the street of my infancy, where I once toddled the hallways banging pots together and screaming "cacophony!"

I stomped out the bidi and reentered the sanctuary, where the PA system was live and waiting. Most of the girls were up in the small balcony now, looking down, or huddled at my feet. I took my place at the altar, lifted the mic and let it screech with feedback.

My voice found its deepest register, found Barry White:

We
oh we better
girl try
try to get ourselves together baby

In the silence after the song, I made my unholy declaration. The words of the lucifer of our hellish town, a fundamental blight on this small slice of Earth. I don't remember exactly what I said, but I know in that moment I felt crushingly male. My neck had grown tree-trunk wide and giraffe long. I embodied the bust. My hair dog-like, my jaw sharp, my cock confident. Behind my smooth dead eyes was the arrogance that I could define freedom, that I could shape the future.

In twenty years, our kid congregation would become professors and parents and authors and global justice advocates. In twenty years, one of us would be dead. In twenty years, the church would remove Thomas Jefferson from its name. If the local deity sees far enough into the future, he sees cracks appearing in his legacy, sees his disciples turning away, cutting ties, severing.

The hard way is the only way men learn.

ANARCHY

I could never decide where to place my anarchy sticker. It came as a freebie with some mail-order CD club shipment, my subscription long-cancelled before they could charge me the initial fee. It stayed on a stack of whatevers in my closet—that unruly red *A*, edges breaking the bounds of its red circle, making the sticker itself sharp. I couldn't stick it on the Wu-Tang skateboard I hadn't learned to ride, because it'd make the Wu-Tang *W* part of a *WA* or an *AW*. Plus, the Wu symbol was already its own act of revolt. I couldn't stick it on the electric bass guitar I hadn't learned to play, because my barely band was a metal band. Our only recorded song was called "Hell Maggots" because a boy I wanted to impress told me to write a song called "Hell Maggots." It wasn't punk at all—it was romantic.

My anarchy was already expressed on a white T-shirt I'd bought at the mall. The back of the T-shirt had "PUNK'S NOT DEAD" in black letters. On the front was the huge red anarchy symbol. I wasn't pulling it off—the *A* felt wrong on the soft, Mom-washed cotton. This symbol was not meant to be commercialized and contained, it was meant to spill out and stretch over some besmirched public surface.

If you scratched the sticker in my closet, it would smell nothing like spray paint. I was the cleanest kid. A freshman.

David Berman, a former Charlottesville resident and UVA radio DJ, once sang:

Punk rock died when the first kid said,
"Punk's not dead. Punk's not dead"

But a few years before he sang that, I showed up to early morning marching band practice in my fucking anarchy T-shirt, with my long hair wet, and my tired brain miserable.

If anarchy was a scratch-and-sniff it'd smell like a bloody nose mixed with morning dew on fresh-mown grass, trampled by the shiny white parade shoes I always "forgot" to bring to football games so that my alternate would have to march in my place.

Our director stood on a ladder above the field and blared orders through his megaphone. "Henry in the clarinets would like you all to know that punk's not dead. Punk is not dead, everyone." When the entire marching band laughs at you, it's time to change your wardrobe. "PUNK'S NOT DEAD" got relegated to sleepshirt status, government overthrow neatly tucked under sheets and snoring.

My literal punkness only expressed itself once a week, and only late at night. Every Thursday around 1AM I'd wake abruptly and turn on my boombox. The new local alternative rock station had a show called *Ska Punks No Losers*, and I'd tune in and crouch by the volume dial, keeping it on the lowest setting—Mom had hearing like the bats that would sometimes erupt out of the basement and flap around our dining room.

Home was getting hard. Mom and I were growing more and more alike, and going for throats. Freshman year was the final full year I'd spend in her house, forever our home. Near the end of our time together, I shaved my head and kicked off two decades of bad hair days. The late Thursday nights would wreck my Friday mornings, but they belonged only to me. I'd rest my head on the bookshelf under the stereo to the whispered shouts of Operation Ivy and "Kids of the Black Hole."

I didn't need to set an alarm for *Ska Punks No Losers*, and it wasn't restless adolescence that pulled me awake in time for the show every Thursday. It was Running Man.

Anarchy is when things take an unexpected turn.

I woke up around 1AM on Thursdays because there were footsteps pounding the street outside my bedroom window, to the dead end then back up: a loud run. In my grogginess it sounded almost inhuman, but I knew it was actually a living legend. Everyone had heard of Running Man, a buff UVA grad who ran upwards of 100 miles each week, often in the latest night or earliest mornings, even in freezing weather. He ran all over city roads and country roads, and had been running for most of my lifetime, fearless. A simple, singular identity, not like the bumper-stickered cars he avoided by running so early, so late.

I was the opposite of a runner. It took me ages to make it around the track because I hated the way the impact made my ridiculous fragile body feel. If you see me running, someone is chasing me. But I'd close my eyes those nights and continue to hear his pounding shoes, close my eyes and imagine I was him, filled with the churning freedom of tearing up and down every road in Charlottesville.

If Running Man was a scratch-and-sniff, he'd smell like moonlit air at midnight.

Running Man was the kind of local character that a college town cultivates. Like the woman downtown who dyed her hair bright colors and dyed her two huge dogs to match. Or the tall woman outside the coffee shop who all the cruel teens called a man. But those characters were hyper-visible; I'd never seen Running Man. My view of the street was blocked by our living room, so I didn't bother pulling open the shutters when he went by. My experience of him stayed strictly auditory.

It seemed like I was the only one who'd never eyed Running Man in the flesh. Friends would tell stories of driving home late from parties and him scaring the hell out them, hustling the other way or blazing past them at a stop sign. One friend paused a movie and hushed everyone to listen to the slap of Running Man's shoes on the pavement outside his house. "It's Running Man, holy shit," he squealed, our sad sack party suddenly charmed, "Have you seen this guy?" He stood up and play-acted as Running Man, describing and demonstrating the full body run, holding his arms out like wings. He took off his shirt. Running Man was famously shirtless, clothed only in short shorts in all seasons. His facial hair was usually unruly and expressive, dangling from his chin and flapping in the wind. I could almost picture it. Then another hush. Running Man ran back by, breathing heavily and making a "hup-hup" noise. We all gave our ears to him.

The sound of Running Man continued to haunt my late nights for a spell, but then his route shifted and my sleep cycle went back to somewhat normal. I grew out of the memory of him, moved away and replaced him with a million New York City characters.

In my late twenties and early thirties, I began having diurnal sleep patterns, waking up in a panic in the middle of the night and surging with insomnia until the early morning when I could quiet my mind and sleep in. When I started waking up, Running Man returned to me. I sometimes thought I could hear him going by outside, even in Los Angeles or some other faraway place. A goofy association. I'd picture him as described to me and smile. By all accounts his presence spread joy—people in town would cheer him on or high-five him or shout encouragement.

At the tail end of December, 2015, I was staying at my in-laws for the holidays. Their house is also in Charlottesville, north of town in a quiet subdivision. I had a diurnal night, an abrupt wakeup, probably around 5AM—not too early— but I couldn't get back to sleep. I was more frustrated by the restlessness because we had a daytrip to Washington DC planned, and I knew I'd have to get my shit together and be out at museums and zoos in the winter weather all day. I watched the hours tick by angrily and a little before 7AM I heard the familiar sound of feet slapping the pavement. *Oh fuck it's Running Man*, I thought, and because this was our hometown, I had hope that it was really him, still at it. I knew I had to finally see the guy. I got out of bed in my pajamas and hustled downstairs, grabbed a topcoat from the hall closet and threw it on, and went outside in the frost and fog and stood barefoot on the chilly porch.

And there was Running Man, as described, short red shorts and topless. He had a knit cap on and a wild gray goatee, thick jacked legs. He wasn't running. He was just standing at the end of my in-laws' driveway. I waved and he turned and ran, lifting his knees and swinging his arms in that legendary way. I knew he was running toward a dead-end. He had to come back by. I thought of going to grab my phone to take his picture but I got worried I'd miss him. I waited a minute. I got cold and went inside and watched from the window, but he didn't return.

In the summer of 2019, I was staying in my old room at Mom's house. I was conceptualizing this book and I looked in my closet and found my little anarchy. There still wasn't a place to stick it. I saw my young punk self in the same mirror. So many things remained, but the boombox was gone. I picked up my phone and cued up the miraculously depressive album that David Berman had just released after a long hiatus. Earlier that week, he'd died by suicide in Brooklyn, where I was preparing to move.

I lay down in the same old bed and remembered Running Man. I googled him. The first page of results was all news headlines, many containing the word "mourn." On the morning of December 29th, 2015—the same morning as our encounter—Running Man was struck by an SUV and died.[1] I scrolled back through the photos on my phone to confirm the date, and found shots of DC art galleries, of upset animals at the zoo. The news story I opened cited the time of the collision "around 7AM,"[2] eerily close to the time I saw him. Only it happened on a stretch of road southwest of town, eight miles away from my in-laws' house.

When I began this chapter, I didn't know it was a ghost story.

BLUEBERRY

Scratch-and-sniffs changed our relationship to all stickers. Once we'd had our first whiff of them, every other sticker was suspect: was this one a scratch-and-sniff? We'd tear at each adhesive with our little nails, huff everything up our developing nostrils, false fruit blending with the smell of rotting picnic tables and the taste of Lunchables. Chemical bliss.

The magic of scratch-and-sniff—of smells emerging from flat nothing—boggled our young minds. But the science was pretty simple. Developed in 1965 by the 3M company as a supplemental use of their microencapsulation technology (normally employed to seal ink on carbonless copy paper), scratch-and-sniff stickers are created by printing tiny, sealed dots of scented oil onto surfaces. When these dots are punctured by a simple scratch, the fragrance they hold is released.[1]

Each scratch-and-sniff had a washed-out aesthetic, perhaps rooted in their 1970s and 80s heyday: their simple illustrations and lightly ridged, alluring surfaces already felt a bit bygone. I have one iconic matte sticker in mind: a bursting basket of blueberries, motion lines popping off the little blue fruits as they tumble out. Printed in bright green letters above: "WILD!" I ate blueberries an hour ago and I couldn't describe what they smell like. But in an instant, in any situation, I can conjure up the scent of a blueberry scratch-and-sniff as if I've just scratched, just lifted it to my nose.

So much of my childhood was recorded. Dad would haul out the bulky VHS video camera and tape us at play or in celebration, toddling and team sports. These tapes are collected in a makeshift museum, the drawers under Mom's TV. Mom never throws any of our things away. This hoarding is connected to her own childhood experience, her own trauma. When she returned home from her long time at the hospital and in rehab after her paralyzing teenage accident, she found that most of her kid possessions were gone— disposed of in the preparation of a ground-floor room for the start of her paraplegic adulthood.

She wouldn't do that to us boys. Our toys and books and games collect dust and will continue to do so, until we decide to go through and dispose of them ourselves, which she always encourages us to do, and which we won't. If we want to fact-check a memory we can easily grab a VHS and confirm. We can watch and find out exactly what we wore, exactly what we shouted at the parent behind the camera. But the smells can't be captured. Their archive exists only in our synapses. We forget but we remember.

In her book *The Future of Nostalgia*, Svetlana Boym describes the nostalgic as someone who "is never a native but a displaced person who mediates between the local and the universal."[2] I identify as a nostalgic. If my Charlottesville was a scratch-and-sniff it'd smell like pine trees, eyeballs, honeysuckle. A synthetic bouquet. My nostalgia isn't for the real thing, the real town, the real childhood.

I opened my nose one morning during Obama's first term and realized My Love's body lotion reminded me of a cereal I used to gobble at Dad's post-divorce house. The cereal was a tie-in for a blockbuster sequel from 1992, a limited-time-only product that vanished from shelves for good in a matter of months. Life was stagnating when I got a whiff of the body lotion, and in stagnation, I tend toward indulgence: I found an unopened box of the cereal for sale on eBay. Grateful to live in the ideal moment for nostalgia addicts, I clicked the "buy it now" option. In three days, I was tearing open the box. A glow-in-the-dark sticker, packed in vacuum-sealed plastic, tumbled into my bowl along with the ancient marshmallows and chocolate Chex.

I poured on almond milk and devoured the stale pile. Bite by bite, the flavors pulled me back in time. I could feel the fructose stunting my growth all over again. A few weeks later I received my master's degree and the next morning I passed out at Six Flags and the park cop referred to me as a "juvenile." My last thought before blacking out was of that undead bowl, that bliss. Every taste was intact, mummified by preservatives.

It's the fake shit that endures.

DEATH TO THE PIXIES

What does it mean when you're in love with the girl who paints "I AM GAY" on the hood of your car and you're also in love with the boy who helps you clean it off?

Me and my friends had just caravanned back to one boy's house after seeing the homoerotic movie where topless men beat the shit out of each other, brand-new driver's licenses burning hot with possibility in our pockets. Our plans were to take off our shirts and beat the shit out of each other, but the movie left us with a different message. Deflated, we took out our aggression on the virtual level instead, mashing buttons on controllers held tight in our laps, watching warriors on the big screen send fountains of blood into the digital air.

One boy lost and walked outside. He shouted for our attention, and we joined him. Scrawled in shoe polish on everyone's cars and shining in the floodlight were the messages, meant to shame: "I ♥ BOYS," "GAY PRIDE," and mine, a simple pronouncement that felt immediately true and inadequate. Our host got his mom and they raided the area under the sink, brought out a bunch of Mr. Yuk-covered bottles. We spent the next hour pouring every available liquid on our hoods and scraping the letters away.

Removing mine felt the most urgent. The other boys owned their graffitied vehicles, but I drove Dad's car: a red Saab with a huge stick shift. I had already done enough damage to it on tricky country driveways, denting the exhaust pipe, spilling Slurpee on the cloth seats. I put myself in Dad's shoes at the moment he'd see the discoloration, the depreciation in value.

If the red Saab was a scratch-and-sniff it'd smell like father like son.

The vandals were probably watching us from behind nearby trees. The girl and boy I loved were a couple, dangerous sweethearts of our high school. This prank was one of many they played on each other. My writhing relationship with my sexuality was collateral damage. Earlier that week I'd watched as the trouble couple attacked each other in the school parking lot and had a pitiless brawl on the concrete. In 1984, that same concrete was marked with the words "SENIORS FOR WHITE SUPREMACY," painted in the wake of racial tensions that followed a school newspaper article on Charlottesville High School's integration, featuring openly racist remarks from anonymous white students. The uproar resulted in the school closing for a day. The graffiti greeted the Black students when they returned, another prank.[1]

As revenge for the shoe polishing, Danger Boy and I stole some girl's car from the school lot, leaving a ransom note in the center of her parking space that said, "You cannot trace us. You cannot find us." As soon as my fellow collateral girl noticed her missing car, I drove her to retrieve it. When the sun hit the hood of the car, my "I AM GAY" glinted. A whisper of the words stayed there until it stopped going in reverse and had to be sold. Mom got me a used, but pristine, white Mazda. I put a dick on it immediately.

The dick was on a bumper sticker that read "Death to the Pixies." The band was newly relevant for their song's needle drop at the end of the topless male shit-beat movie. On the sticker, the band's front man is naked on his knees with his head on the ground, his ass turned up in the air. One of his hands extends forward, gripped in a fist, and from a distance it seems like he's giving the thumbs-down gesture. But on closer inspection the thumb is really his dick. I parked it with pride.

I didn't start this chapter early enough. It starts with the Russian Revolution.

On July 17th 1918, in the cellar of a house in the Urals, The Grand Duchess Anastasia Romanov, along with her four siblings and her parents—Czar Nicholas II and Alexandra— were gunned down, stabbed, and burned. Their remains were doused in sulfuric acid and buried in a mine shaft.

65 years later, when I was born, Anastasia was miraculously alive and screaming out the window of a cat-infested house four blocks away. Anna, her assumed name, had been rescued from a Berlin canal in 1920, following a suicide attempt. After two years of recovery, she announced that she was secretly Anastasia, spared from the execution that

befell the rest of her family and spirited away by a Bolshevik soldier. She spent the ensuing decades living in Europe with sympathetic czarists and believers, defending her legitimacy. Her story inspired plays and films. A private investigation proved she was in fact a missing Polish-German factory worker, but many stuck by her claims, loyal believers.[2] In 1968 she did the relatively mundane act of marrying a UVA professor and settling down in Charlottesville.

Fifteen years later, regardless of the truth of her identity, she and her husband were unofficially the queen and king of local quirk. They shuffled around town, regaling anyone who'd listen with stories, and filled their home with hoarded potatoes, animals, and take-out containers. (Anna, in her paranoia, refused to eat from metal.) Their neighbors filed complaints about the mess and the noise and the smell. In the fall of my first year, Anna was committed to a mental institution.[3]

A month later, Anna's husband fired up their old trash-packed station wagon, bribed an attendant, and broke his wife out. For the next three days they drove around the county, eating junk food and eluding a multi-state police alert. They were apprehended in their broken-down car in front of an abandoned house an hour south of town. Anna was returned to the hospital, and shortly after, the death she'd mythically evaded for so long finally found her.[4]

I thought of their final drive—gods of aimless escape—as I drove my dick-stickered car with my beloved Danger Boy in the passenger seat. I squinted to scan the dark country road, and he told me his brilliant idea: "We should strap flashlights to the hood so we can see where we're going." I turned on the headlights. "Let's see who's up," he demanded. The plan was to cruise past the house of everyone we knew, his favorite practice.

I was never more Charlottesville than when I was driving around town, aimless in the forgotten hours of night, channeling the Grand Duchess, avoiding my destination, my fate. Driving past the house of scolding and the house of spin-the-bottle and the house of just experimenting; past the home of the brain surgeon who saved Superman's life when he fell from a horse; past the balcony where the future governor would sit and shoot squirrels with a rifle; past the fiefdom of car dealerships on the hill overlooking the city; past the sign with the missing *C* that says "Welcome to harlottesville;" through the intersection where the car in the high speed pursuit flipped over the guard rail and sheared off my acting coach's roof; past the spot where some classmates beat up a UVA student; past the spot where my neighbor's son shot himself; past the spot where my friend's martial arts teacher stabbed himself; past the park that hosted the yearly carnival and then hosted the Nazi rally; past the pedophile's house and the pedophile's house and the house the guy burned down; past the house of the National Book Award winner and sexual predator; every winding street a vine knotted with thorns, with men; past one Thomas Jefferson after another; past *For Sale* and *Slow Children Crossing* and *No Outlet* and *Parking Reserved Funeral Today* and *Playground Closes at Dusk*; past the houses of the dead, who I'd been mourning by looking at

Google Street View, imagining that when these photos were captured, the people I'd lost were still alive inside; past the bar where the cops broke a man's nose on the pavement, or threw a man over a railing, or arrested a man when he tried to intervene; past the burned-out squad car on the hill with the sign above it that read "LAW ENFORCEMENT IS OUT OF CONTROL: KARUPT;" past the nearby stoplight where the women pulled up alongside me and screamed, "you can't go up there, faggot, it's private property;" past the now-demolished dorm where I learned to reclaim the word queer— as a theory, as an incantation toward sense-making, belonging; driving away, and further away, through a blizzard of small, destructive choices, crossing the Downtown Mall and crossing the Downtown Mall and crossing the Downtown Mall.

I parked in the high school lot. It was suddenly 2019. I stepped out of a new car, my Mazda and its dick lost to time. I'd come to visit the memorial garden that students had dedicated to an old friend, who'd returned home a few years before to teach English as a second language at our alma mater, and who'd recently passed away from cancer.

A wall of opulent graffiti greeted me—"ABOLISH ICE" and "ABOLISH CAPITALISM" and "BLACK LIVES MATTER"—and there, in glorious yellow: "BE GAY DO CRIME."

PINK CIRCLE

The first time I entered the video store there was sperm on the TV. Chattering white tadpoles swarmed through a glowing pink tunnel, "I Get Around" by The Beach Boys blasting. A single sperm with the voice of Bruce Willis wiggled its way through the outer layer of an egg. I had no idea what I was getting into.

My parents set me loose to comb the kids' section. I couldn't watch the same three movies they'd taped— *Spaceballs*, *Superman II*, and *Claymation Christmas*—over and over again anymore. I'd already memorized every static-filled commercial break.

If a video store in the 90s was a scratch-and-sniff it'd smell like a kid in a candy shop.

I chose *The Last Unicorn* and that became my go-to. I'd rent it every week and pop it in the VHS player, sitting rapt like the experience was brand new. If it was rented out before we got there, I'd get jealous of the person who'd deprived me of my ritual, wonder who were they and how dare they.

As I grew, the video store grew with me, and together we crested the peak era of home entertainment. The store changed ownership and moved to a new location, a second floor up a flight of carpeted stairs. For ease, the clerks left a wicker basket on a rope inside the door for video return, and they'd pulley it up to the counter above, like maidens in a tower. I needed to be one of these maidens. I stopped wanting to drive a taxi for a living and started wanting to work in a video store. I was 9. It's still all I want to do.

Ten years later, my dream came true. I returned home from my freshman year of film school in New York and applied. The video store was looking to hire more clerks to help with the transition from VHS to DVD. The owner snapped me up. He was a bighearted no-bullshitter from Queens with a close-cropped Shi-tzu and a house plastered floor-to-ceiling in Broadway posters. His magnificence spilled out into the store and we employees helped make it all to his liking. We painted stars and film reels and yellow brick roads on the floor. We tacked up cardboard standees and lobby cards. Old movie paraphernalia dripped from every wall, a rainforest of obsolescence.

We trafficked in the tangible. We touched every new release that came through the door, cracking their cases like oysters and giving them new shells, plastic on plastic on plastic. We blessed each with a circular sticker, color-coded for the geographic section where they belonged: blue for America, red for Europe, pink for Asia and Oceania. We slid the newly stickered DVDs alongside their flabby VHS doppelgängers, peopling the documentary section, the television section, the gay & lesbian section, the theater section and the independent section, which were also the gay & lesbian sections.

I came in early every morning to open up. I savored the thud of tapes falling through the after-hours return slot and onto the floor, stickers like confetti. I rented porn to my former teachers, picked out TV shows for a dying friend to binge. A local rock musician in her third trimester dressed me down for a bad recommendation. My shrink made small talk and tried to lie to her son about how she knew me. There was a deep intimacy between us all, because I held their rental history at my fingertips. Every title they'd taken home was logged in our computer system, and I could call it up with a simple click. Surveillance masquerading as care. I reminded our elderly customers which murder mysteries they'd already checked out, sitting regal at my desk, enforcing the late fees which paid my salary. It was the best and only job. I shed all ambition, because I could.

I got my education after closing, using my free rentals to stockpile films and tear through them on my laptop in my childhood bedroom. I learned more in a sleepless evening than in four years of film school—learned Jarman and Fassbinder and *Priscilla Queen of the Desert*; learned Charles Burnett and *Double D Nurses in Love* and *The Czech is in the Male*; learned Araki and Ozu and *Paris is Burning*; learned Lizzie Borden. A barely-audible bootleg VHS of Todd Haynes' *Superstar: The Karen Carpenter Story*—his tragic biopic told with barbie dolls—became *The Last Unicorn* of my adulthood.

The first time I entered what would become my New York video store, I noticed a clipping from *The Onion* taped up behind the counter: "Film-School Graduate Goes Straight to Video Store Job." I was there to open an account; the next disc of a show was taking too long to arrive in the mail from Netflix. I had just graduated with a degree in film and TV production. I asked the clerk for an application.

If a video store in the 2000s was a scratch-and-sniff it'd smell like a collapsing star.

The next week, they hired me and handed me a gun. The gun was full of stickers—it printed numbers on them so I could fire prices onto our retail DVDs. I placed them on high shelves to either side of the store, using a grabber to reach—the same familiar grabber Mom had at home. The New York video store was spartan, functional: one large room with troughs where our card catalog was filed with paper advertisements for the tapes and DVDs, and the actual inventory kept in the back, on rows of steel library stacks. Beyond the stacks the building went deeper, to the office where our boss hung out, and stairs down to what we called the murder basement, where lord knows what was stored.

It was different being a clerk in New York. We worked among the stars. We could have 30-minute conversations about Czech cinema with the Bond villain who crushes men to death with her thighs, or get a private serenade from Björk and her daughter. In my hometown store there was no upward mobility, but in New York some of us would ascend. One day I'd watch the lowkey couch-surfer sing on a jumbotron as his band headlined the Hollywood Bowl. I'd watch the hyperactive high schooler win the Golden Globe for best actress in a motion picture comedy or musical. I didn't have their momentum. I was already where I had hoped to be.

My paradise was shaken by a confrontation with a shoplifter. I saw him slyly knock down some shrink-wrapped DVDs and tuck them in his jacket, and I rushed to the door to call him out. The day manager—a masterclass in unpleasantness—didn't have my back. She sat at the desk ignoring the situation. The shoplifter denied everything, spat at me and rushed away. I retreated to the cramped bathroom and had a panic attack. I sat on the toilet and realized I was still holding my pricing gun. I used it to sticker the front of my shirt, shooting one after another onto my chest, marking myself down. If my phone at the time could have taken video, I would have recorded it.

When my shift ended and I left, still shaking, I noticed a man loitering on the bench out front, smoking a long cigarette, as if in wait. He was old but dressed young, in a weathered flat-cap and a baggy button-up. I crossed the street, stopped and turned around, saw him shuffle inside the store, watched through the bright window as he stepped behind the counter, opened the cash register, removed a few twenties, and walked back outside.

The following day, he was behind the counter when I showed up. We were introduced. This was Paul. He'd worked at the store since before I was born. He smelled like wet newspapers and seemed to melt into the walls. I heard more about him when he wasn't present.

In younger days, he was a hugely influential music critic. He introduced Dylan to folk music via his magazine and his record collection, was briefly Bowie's publicist, and had saved Warren Zevon's life by getting him to sober up while writing a profile for *Rolling Stone*.[1] His celebrity-scraping career was in the past. "I don't really want a job anymore where you have to think," he'd said to an interviewer in 2000.[2] Amen. Paul was the inverse of my co-workers who were on a path to stardom. He'd come back down to earth. The fridge of his apartment on the Upper East Side was stocked only with Cokes and Reese's peanut butter cups. A few times a week he would trek down to the store and simply hang around, not working, just being. A fading dream of an employee, a projection of my possible future, the ultimate clerk.

He would sneak money from the register or from the cashbox in the office when he thought no one was watching. I don't know why I was always watching, but I assumed this was his back-pay, compensation for being a human talisman, sustained and protected from death by the video store, another entity on its way out. When I casually mentioned Paul's skimming to the boss, he acted surprised. From then on there was a code to open the register, and the cashbox was hidden. I watched Paul fumble with the locks, search the office in vain. I was working longer and longer hours, pulling full day-to-night double shifts, trying to become a permanent fixture. The boss took pity on me, asked if I was okay, opened the register and gave me hundreds of dollars. He thought I must have been catastrophically hard up for cash. In actuality I had just been introduced to the extent of my generational wealth. A check had arrived—dividends from a family partnership—that covered my entire year's rent. I was given control of six-figure stock holdings. My work frenzy was avoidance—an attempt to do nothing different, to accelerate the sameness. I gave Paul my unearned cash bonus and decided to quit.

On my final shift, at closing time, two irregular customers dawdled too long. To give them the hint, I turned up my music so loud it shook the window glass. The customers approached and said, "Can you turn it down?" And I said, "We're closed," and they said, "Can you turn it down?" and I turned it up and they stormed out and I was God.

Paul died a month later. His body went undiscovered for weeks.

In the summer of 2007, the same month that the New York video store closed—sold off and refurbished into a boutique, the murder basement converted into a glitzy lower floor—I walked the property of my aunt and uncle's new vineyard in Sonoma. They showed me the plot of land where they were going to build a house. My uncle was on the Netflix Board of Directors. He told me that the company was starting to produce original content. The aggregator tracking every subscriber's streaming activity had shown Netflix that people mostly viewed British TV dramas, movies directed by David Fincher, and movies starring Kevin Spacey. In response, they'd acquired the rights to remake a British TV drama, hired David Fincher to direct, and hired Kevin Spacey to star. A perfect formula. We stared down into the valley that would soon be a septic system.

The Charlottesville video store of my youth clung to life for seven more years. I popped in to catch up whenever I was in town to holiday or teach, checking out stacks of titles to screen for my class, supporting their survival campaign, a David to the Goliath of streaming giants. The Last Video Store.

If the Last Video Store was a scratch-and-sniff it'd smell like an aging wolf that's left its pack to go and lie down and rot alone.

The fate of the store's collection was the final sticking point, and when the UVA library struck a deal to acquire around 10,000 titles, the man from Queens held a sell-off of redundant inventory. I darted straight to the bootleg of *Superstar: The Karen Carpenter Story*, couldn't believe my luck that it was still on the shelf. I brought it home, left the sticker on. I didn't even own a VHS player anymore. I found a high-definition version on YouTube, and held the physical version in my arms as I watched. I missed stickering until my fingers ached, missed standing around eating jars of dry-roasted peanuts and talking about movies all fucking day. I missed being a dying breed, an aorta of Charlottesville culture. Our function clogged, slowed and stopped, and with us passed the era. Too late and too soon.

HEART

The heart sticker we all know is not shaped like the anatomical human heart. The shape of the true human heart is too unruly to outline and grasp at a young age, so it was the iconic letter-V-with-a-top-butt that I held at my kid fingertips to stick on valentines for everyone in class. Some of them had eyes and mouths—humanoid hearts with the potential to contain their own hearts. False hearts all the way down. I carried this icon within me. If you dumped me, that's what would be split in two. If you cut me open, that cute pumping symmetry would greet you.

There are multiple theories about when, and why, this heart symbol emerged and became dominant. It might have first been molded onto Cyrenian coins in the seventh century BC, the shape mimicking the seed-pod of the now-extinct silphium plant, fabled as a contraceptive, and so associated with fucking.[1] Then the further stretch, the association of fucking with love. Or to balance the profane with the sacred, the symbol represented the heart of Jesus, surrounded by thorns in a revelation experienced by Saint Margaret Mary Alacoque in the 1600s, and proliferated, like so many icons, first with the Catholic Church and then by greeting card corporations. [2]

If the heart was a scratch-and-sniff it'd smell like a pharmacy on fire.

As an adult I have a recurring dream: Mom dies and I inherit a ring. The ring is a pink crystal heart—her heart.

The summer I moved to Los Angeles, I took a nap in the middle of unpacking. I woke to a phone call from Mom, the tone of her voice loaded—bad news. Another accident, this time in my extended family.

The next few days and weeks and months were full of panic and updates and sleeplessness, overwhelmed with feelings of far away. The shape of the story didn't fully form until that December, when I'd travelled east to Mom, swapped out heart stickers for gift wrap, and driven to the deep south.

Normally, my Alabama aunt breaking her ankle in a chipmunk hole while taking out the compost on Christmas Eve wouldn't even register. My family has mastered the art of getting injured. But that year my Alabama aunt's mishap was heavenly. It made our Christmas gathering perfect, the best ever.

Five Months before, her son—my cousin—was biking by himself, in Chicago, at sunset. A semi-trailer cut a corner too close and my cousin went under its back-right wheels. A full crush, the ER called it, his middle decimated.

This was not our family's first encounter with the viciousness of vehicles, but it was the first for this generation. We cousins were scattered all over America, far from the folks in Alabama. Alabama, where Mom was injured, when she was even younger than my cousin, when she was a cheerleader for her high school. She went out the window of a car on the way back from a basketball game, and as the car careened into a ditch, it landed on top of her. Mom was the first to be injured and has been for the longest. She is the matron saint of our family's misfortune, canonized by survival, her wheelchair a holiday staple. Uncle Fred.

When my cousin was run over, a message center erupted from the south, keeping everyone posted on his condition. He had to be resuscitated three times during the night, but was then decidedly stable. Everyone in his immediate family headed to be by his side for the reconstructive surgeries. When I heard the details of the damage, delivered to me by Mom as I sat up groggy in my un-moved-into Los Angeles apartment, I assumed, like what happened to her, that my cousin would never walk again.

The newer wheelchairs my Alabama family has collected aren't named. They can't hope to stand out as individuals. Over the fall before our Christmas gathering, we collected even more immobility. Granmamma acquired a motorized scooter after she'd had a few too many early evening falls.

So many of our elders had their share of disability; my cousin became the forerunner for our generation. He was no longer at the kid's table with the rest of us. And on that Christmas we had a record number of wheelchairs present. When my Alabama aunt stepped out into the crisp—not cold—air the night before, she had no idea she'd soon be a last-minute addition to the wheelchair lineup. She was using my cousin's wheelchair, because, miraculously, he didn't need it. He could do with a sleek cane, and could stride into the living room, and we could applaud.

That year, injury was so fresh and constant that none of us needed to talk about it. No insult was added. Some of us chattered about how accurate a new movie was in depicting the circumstances of our southern childhoods. Some of us had a problem with that sentiment.

My cousin stood in front of the fire. We all sat, wheels locked, hands on armrests. Nobody read from anything. We read each other's faces instead, as my cousin finally spoke. The story of an angel, but not the one we'd heard every year. His story. The angel that came to him in that broken moment, as he lay on the Chicago concrete. He hadn't hit his head, but the pain removed most of his memory. When he regained consciousness in the hospital bed, all he recalled of the crush was an angelic figure crouched over him, arms out in the city lights, telling him it was going to be alright.

A few days after the collision and the surgery, the angel arrived in my cousin's hospital room; he'd tracked him down. Just to check up. His name was Art, and he had been standing on the corner right by the collision. Art ran to my cousin, had someone call an ambulance, got information on how to contact our family, kept others from moving him, saved his life.

This became our new Christmas story. We were all little kids in my cousin's narrative thrall.

He told us about his planned tattoo, to be inked right over his heart, beside the chest-covering scar. The word "heart"— not the symbol—with "art" in parentheses; something permanent for someone real. My aunt couldn't give her standard motherly plea against it.

FIRE DANCER

The defining anthem of Charlottesville is a song called "I Hate Charlottesville." It begins:

> *This is about the love and hate relationship*
> *between me and Charlottesville*
> *I like people*
> *I like nature here*
> *but I have nowhere to go out tonight*

The song was written by Atsushi Miura, owner of a local sushi bar that also housed a music venue in its grubby, low-ceilinged basement. Atsushi would take the stage after shows with an acoustic guitar and harmonica and perform his anthem, a concluding gesture throughout the late 90s and early 2000s.[1] Its wailed chorus:

> *I hate Charlottesville*
> *too boring*
> *I hate Charlottesville*
> *nothing*

The venue was one of the least boring things about Charlottesville. Literally and figuratively underground, at one end of an insignificant strip mall, it hosted goth nights, local noise acts, and a staggering roster of touring musicians who are legends now, bands I would have killed to see, who at the time only drew college or hip townie crowds. I missed out on the whole happening—too young, and then too agoraphobic—but I ate at the sushi bar every other week for most of middle school. After the divorce it was Dad's go-to spot for our Wednesday visitation meal. We'd remove our shoes and sit on the floor of the restaurant's elevated platform, our feet in the trench below the table. I'd scarf tuna rolls and tempura, feel international. We'd always leave well before the venue opened its doors, before the floor began to rumble. Before Atsushi would appear and croon:

One day a friend of mine came to Charlottesville
to be entertained
I took him to Monticello and walked around UVA
then I had nowhere to show
so I took him to some restaurant
then the friend hesitatingly said
can I go home?

The only Charlottesville sticker with a global reach is the fire dancer. It represents Dave. I didn't want to write about Dave in this book, but here we are. Dave and his band were and will probably remain the most famous musicians from Charlottesville. The fire dancer—a skinny female-ish figure with arms extended in a Christ-like pose, one leg lifted and bent, ass pronounced, no head—was drawn by Dave himself, to represent their ecstatic audience. I was not their audience. The smoke-drenched boomer bar on the Downtown Mall where Dave got his start felt diametrically opposed to the sushi basement. Dave and his band made the kind of inoffensive music almost everyone could agree on, from parents to peers. It wasn't for me. Nothing resonated.

They amassed a Grateful Dead-level following. The fire dancer became their brand, like the Dead's bear. I realized that Dave had blown up when my bunkmate at camp mentioned him. This boy came from a few states away, and when he heard I was from Charlottesville he started to sing a Dave song. He was holding my knees while I did sit-ups. I was trying not to sweat because I wanted to stay pretty for the boy. It was the first year I felt pretty, and the last. Something about how my lips looked, lots of biting. Before puberty ate me alive.

I told two stories about Dave throughout my teens and early adulthood. One is about how I was momentarily more famous, or at least more newsworthy. Dave played a small Mother's Day festival on the lawn of the hippie private school, and the next morning Mom and I made the cover of the paper, not him. In the picture our faces are painted and pressed close together. We represented the occasion, the love between a mother and child. This story makes me feel better about myself.

The other is about how I almost hit Dave with my car. I was pulling out of a parking lot near UVA and was watching the traffic, not the sidewalk, when Dave walked across the lip of the driveway. I slammed on the brakes and nudged him slightly with my bumper, and he placed one hand on the hood of my car. We locked eyes. I thought, "Oh hey it's Dave," and he thought, "Fuck this kid whoever he is." And he kept walking and I kept trying to drive. I joked that I would never wash the handprint off the hood. Whenever I tell this story, I'm lying. It actually happened to Dad. Dad was the driver and the almost-hitter. It's okay if this makes you doubt the veracity of my memoir.

Dave's music became part of the general ambience. His songs would soundtrack our kid parties in unfinished basements, where we'd gnaw on each other, until I got the chance to switch to a Mariah Carey CD. His voice would bellow out across camp dances, following me and a boy as we led our dates to the lower tennis court, coupling up four feet apart in the almost invisible night, kissing the girls and their braces. When the girls hurried back to their cabins, Dave was still in the air as the boy and I closed the gap and kept the kiss going without them, no braces between us.

If the fire dancer was a scratch-and-sniff it'd smell like the red "RECORD" light of a video camera in the woods.

I can't talk about Charlottesville—the town it was or that it became—without talking about Dave, and that's because of Corn. Corn was Dave's manager, and brokered their shared success into a music industry empire. I call him Corn because my stepmom pronounces his name that way. "I work for Corn." "She works for Corn, too." It seemed like lots of people were employed by Corn. Besides the music companies, Corn also became a prominent real estate developer, buying up shuttered warehouses and vacant lots along West Main Street, with plans to build high-rise apartment buildings.[2] He created new or refurbished concert venues that attracted major touring acts, and owned bars and restaurants that brought in chefs from major cities. Locals joked that they received their paychecks from Corn and then gave the money right back to him when they went out on the weekend.[3] His holdings were shots of adrenaline into the night life of a sleepy college town grown stale.

The final verse of I Hate Charlottesville asks:

Oh Mr. Jefferson
is this what you expected to see?
Did you freeze this town
in the 19th century?

In local mythology, Dave was a hero who walked among us. A global diplomat for Charlottesville. His foundation contributed to a diverse range of charities and community initiatives. When I was in high school, UVA expanded and renovated its football stadium, a partial motivation being that afterwards Dave and his band would return for a triumphant hometown show, now that the enlarged venue could handle his crowd, the fire dancers themselves.

In contrast, the conventional wisdom around Corn was that he'd bought the town. He drew comparisons to the repulsive reality star and future president. Corn the capitalist supervillain, Dave the hairless cat in his lap. His actions often fit the part. He planted a bourgeois restaurant in the middle of a lower-income neighborhood. He lived on a white-columned estate outside of town. He managed a band called Lady Antebellum.

As a flesh-and-blood human, Corn was elusive. I still don't know what he looks like. I might have bumped into him countless times at the bagel place. Instead of looking him up, I just pictured him as a humongous ear of corn. Though his proximity to fame gives him prominence and makes him a target, he's only one in a large crop of Charlottesville real estate speculators.

The new millennium sees an influx of changes, and every time I return home there are areas I barely recognize: gentrified neighborhoods become dining districts; subdivisions and homogenous apartment complexes sprawl in all directions, replacing fields and woodlands; a grandiose hotel begins construction at the center of the Downtown Mall, but then ceases, its skeleton standing unbuilt for decades, overgrown with vines. The cost-of-living soars well above the national average.

If Corn was a scratch-and-sniff he'd smell like scaffolding.

His developments are aimed at me. I've got money to burn. I live in New York or Los Angeles most of the year. When I return to Charlottesville, I can indulge in similar crap. I get dinner at his high-end sushi restaurant, overlooking the Downtown Mall. The contradictions of corn. Our bodies can't digest it fully. Again and again, Charlottesville lands on desirable lists: most beautiful southern towns, best foodie cities, best places to live until you die.

And Atsushi sings:

a magazine said
this is one of the dream small towns
yes this is a town to dream
forever

In 2004, three things happened. Atsushi sold his restaurant and left town. While crossing a bridge in Chicago, one of Dave's tour buses dumped 800 pounds of human waste into the river, drenching the passengers on a sightseeing boat below.[4] My brother played me a recording of "I Hate Charlottesville." It resonated.

BE NICE TO ME I GAVE BLOOD TODAY

A handful of years ago, the person I hated most in the world died. Her life ended in the small Alabama town where Mom grew up. I read the short obituary my grandparents had sent and learned nothing but her name. I found her on Facebook and the first post on her wall was from Mom:

"Burn in Hell."

There's one sticker I don't deserve to wear. It's typically in the shape of a heart and it says, "Be nice to me I gave blood today!" As soon as I turned seventeen, Mom wanted me to give blood. It was a noble, generous act, and besides, she was alive because of blood donors. Their gifts had saved her life as a teenager, and then regularly throughout her adulthood, during continuing surgeries and emergencies and anemia. "It's most important that *you* give," she said, "because you're the universal donor." My whole life she'd reminded me that my blood type was O negative, rare and transfusable to anyone. When I felt like there was nothing else good about my pimpled body, my baseline of self-esteem was my blood type, its generosity to the world, to my mother. The universal donor.

I'd never refused Mom any request, always at the ready to reach, or to clean up, or to rescue in a random disaster. But still—like any child—when a parent told me what to do with my life, my body, the part that belonged to just me, my impulsive thought was always *No, not ever*. My hypochondria had emerged with my facial hair. I'd lie on the top bunk at Dad's and torture myself with episodes of *ER*, checking my pulse every five minutes. I was afraid of my own blood, afraid what it would do if it was added to someone else. Fearmongering around HIV/AIDS was constant in my boyhood, taunted and used to terrify. The specter of contagion was present in the fleeting encounters I'd had, with whoever of whatever gender. From 1985-2015, there was a lifetime ban on donating—instituted by the FDA—for men who had sex with other men.[1] I never went far enough to be asked the question, never went far enough to answer "yes." By 17, I was already dating the person I'm still in a monogamous relationship with. So, Mom never asked the question either. I didn't react well to losing blood, or having it taken. Even during routine draws, a sense of doom overwhelmed me and I passed out. The fasting didn't help. "You don't have to fast when you donate," Mom says, "and they give you a cookie." I wasn't interested in a cookie. I was addicted to this defiance.

The sticker I see in the nightmares where I disappoint my mother is a cartoon blood drop, with eyes, legs, arms, and

Mickey Mouse hands. He's giving me the thumbs up, and would be giving the thumbs up to whoever was facing me, if I ever earned the right to wear it.

Whenever we encountered a senseless tragedy, which was often, Mom would remind me to give blood. One Virginia summer we drove by a roadside sign: "Slow down for Sydney." I told Mom about the tractor-trailer driver who'd killed 16-year-old Sydney, when he ran a red light and collided with her car on her way to school. I asked, "how could you live with yourself after something like that?" Mom said, "the woman who caused my accident never once apologized." I said, "yeah, but you didn't die." Mom forced silence on us for the rest of the drive.

The woman who never once apologized, the person I hated most in the world, was The Driver on that early 70s January night, ferrying Mom and the other cheerleaders home from an away game. Speeding. Mom doesn't bring up The Driver much. She fades into the background of evocations of "my accident" or "my injury." I got trickles of information over the years, on rides between our condo in Birmingham and my grandparents' house—the house Mom grew up in, then came back to from the hospital as a teenager, newly paralyzed for life. Even though the highway hadn't been built back then, I imagined that it was the very stretch of road The Driver drove off of, that every ditch below was the ditch where Mom ended up, crushed.

I pictured the scene, the shoulder where the cops questioned The Driver, where she said she'd been in a rush because she was fighting with her husband, where she made excuses, where she didn't once say sorry. It all gets conflated into a rainy, terrifying night. A turning point. The eldest daughter of a prominent family, laid low. This narrative from Mom's youth was so different from how my brother and I viewed her disability. It was all we'd ever known. To my brother and me, there was no before to Mom's after; our life with Fred was entirely normal, no tragedy involved. But we accepted Mom's reality, understood there was a villain somewhere in the past.

"I'm just glad my parents won't run into her at the grocery store anymore," Mom said when we learned of The Driver's death. I didn't know how to respond. I recommended a TV show about punishment and redemption in a small southern town. Recommendations are our love language.

I try to empathize with The Driver. What would her apology have changed? I understand that forgiveness is not an option for Mom, for the part of her left behind in high school, always hurt. One night at her hometown country club, Mom spotted another cheerleader who'd been in The Driver's car. I watched Mom revert, the club transforming into a high school cafeteria. Her eyes darting, feeling distortedly seen, the air thick with old grudges. Forgiving The Driver would have been a monumental task, especially for a forever teenager.

I see new opportunities for forgiveness come and go during my lifetime. New villains. My father, who betrays, who leaves. The doctors, who further injure Mom during a botched surgery. And me, the universal donor, choosing to withhold his blood from those in need. Unforgiven, all.

I was well into my thirties when I glanced at a medical document from my birth. My weight after being C-sectioned out, and there, on a thin line, my blood type: O+. Positive, not negative. Mom had called me the wrong type all along. For a moment, I felt like I was let off the hook—no longer as needed, no longer shirking some cosmic duty, no longer universal—but the relief didn't last. I still couldn't forgive myself for all those missed blood drives, couldn't let go of the sticker I wasn't worthy of wearing. Forgiveness doesn't run in our veins.

If our blood was a scratch and sniff, it'd smell like ivy in the yard, like an artificial fireplace, like microwave nachos, like dehumidifiers, like Mentholatum, like fever dreams where our hands are too big to hold our little books, like icing squeezed out of a tube onto toaster pastries, like metal buttons to open doors, like a heating pad, like a crepuscular Oldsmobile, like chicken livers from the KFC drive-thru, like mouth-scalding coffee that's somehow never hot enough, like audiobooks of cozy cat mysteries and graphic horse breeding, like the waterfalls by the highway around Chattanooga, like potato chips (but just the foldy ones), like Jack Russell terriers, like the dry dead grass of the Deep South, like an Alabama lake after a tornado, like puddles of gasoline and fresh rain, like thunder bouncing off the 23rd floor of a Manhattan apartment tower, like every crack in the sidewalk that others avoid stepping on to spare their mothers' backs and that I roll Mom right over, like inherited trauma, like a tense present.

The year The Driver died, I helped Mom clean up her blood. Little spurts from an unnoticed and unfelt toe cut had sprinkled every few feet, down the hallway of our house and into my bedroom. The splotches had dried on the hardwood, deep ruby medallions that resembled wax seals. We were home.

ARE YOU TRIGGERED?

A pickup truck barrels through a crosswalk and honks hard at the pedestrians who've just leapt to safety. I'm one of them. An American flag and a Confederate flag flap above the truck's bed. A series of letter stickers form a white arc on the back window: "ARE YOU TRIGGERED?"

The answer is yes. One year ago, I was diagnosed with PTSD. The word triggered has become a funny thing for certain people to lob at other people. The Are You Triggered Truck honks again, a performance for no one and everyone, emboldened and supported from on high.

It's June of 2017. We're five months into the fascist presidency. I'm back in Charlottesville. The Are You Triggered Truck is a harbinger, heralding the white supremacists emerging from the woodwork of town or parading in from other parts of the country. They've come to defend the statues.

One hundred years ago, before the invention of the adhesive sticker, those fucks with the Confederacy deep in their hearts instead adhered their garish hate to the earth with bronze and concrete. A local white supremacist benefactor—whose name is associated with many elements of Charlottesville, including the sprawling park where Mom always took little me to play—commissioned the statues of Robert E. Lee and Stonewall Jackson for the downtown area. They were completed in the 1920s, assurances to everyone— most expressly the Black citizens living emancipated lives nearby—that the exaltation of the Confederacy was alive and well. The Klan attended the unveilings and celebrated, recruited.[1]

Writes W.E.B Du Bois in a 1931 issue of *The Crisis*:

> The most terrible thing about War, I am convinced, is its monuments, the awful things we are compelled to build in order to remember the victims. In the South, particularly, human ingenuity has been put to it to explain on its war monuments, the Confederacy. Of course, the plain truth of the matter would be an inscription something like this: "Sacred to the memory of those who fought to Perpetuate Human Slavery." But that reads with increasing difficulty as time goes on. It does, however, seem to be overdoing the matter to read on a North Carolina Confederate monument: "Died Fighting for Liberty!"[2]

A paternal ancestor of mine left New England early in the 19th century to seek his fortune in Alabama, where he started several businesses which relied on the labor of enslaved people. In the aftermath of his Civil War defeat, he wrote a letter to his father, a Connecticut abolitionist. In the letter he pleads: "Can we be allowed to be men again?" In the name of unity and national healing, America nursed the bruised ego of the white southerner. Over the next half-century of perpetual white supremacy, 780 Confederate monuments were erected. Eighty counties and cities and 103 K-12 schools bore the names of prominent members of the Confederacy.

For almost my entire tenure in grade school, we got the third Monday of January off to honor Lee-Jackson-King Day. Since the beginning of the 1900s in Virginia, Lee and Jackson had been celebrated on this day, and for hard-to-parse reasons, in 1984 Virginia shifted the recently established Martin Luther King Day to the same day which celebrated those who fought for the continued enslavement of his people. The legislative rhetoric around the offensive mashup was that all three were "defenders of causes." Lee-Jackson-King. It rolled off our kid tongues when we talked about what we were doing with our extended weekends. Like all acts of Confederate re-inscription, this one directly coincided with, and sabotaged, an acknowledgement of Black life. The racist generals wouldn't be removed from Dr. King's holiday until 2000.[3]

In 2016, a Charlottesville High School student named Zyahna Bryant started a petition calling for the Lee statue's removal. City council member and vice mayor Wes Bellamy also championed the cause, and a commission was created to explore removing both Confederate statues from downtown. In February of 2017, the council voted in favor of removal.[4]

The actions of these Black activists were met with anything but unanimous local support, with many condemning them as divisive. This became a flashpoint—compounded by the grotesquerie of the fascist president's rise—in which a city was confronted with the long-standing ugliness beneath its polished identity. For a substantial contingent of white Charlottesville, acts of reparation are uncomfortable and burdensome. Afraid to peel the stickers for fear of the residue they'll leave behind.

Du Bois, *The Crisis*, 1928:

> What Lee did in 1861, other Lees are doing in 1928. They lack the moral courage to stand up for justice to the Negro because of the overwhelming public opinion of their social environment. Their fathers in the past have condoned lynching and mob violence, just as today they acquiesce to the disenfranchisement of educated and worthy black citizens, provide wretchedly inadequate public schools for Negro children and endorse a public treatment of sickness, poverty and crime which disgraces civilization.[5]

As a white person in a land of white power, I had the privilege of forgetting the statues existed, could let them fade into the background, normalize. But they were always beacons.

When these beacons are threatened, their stewards descend with torches to relight.

The first gathering to protect the Lee statue happened in May, led by a Neo-Nazi and UVA graduate who will be eternally famous for getting punched in the face on live TV by an antifascist hero. The Neo-Nazi's creepy vigil laid the groundwork for another racist UVA grad to plot something bigger for August, a rally to unite the right. It fits that former students of Jefferson's University would feel a welcome mat laid out for their sneering white supremacy, having inhabited the academical village created by and enshrining a man for whom freedom wasn't imaginable without enslavement, for whom exploration wasn't possible without genocide.

The Are You Triggered Truck swerves left and leaves my sight, tearing across the Downtown Mall and toward the bronze hooves of Lee's horse. Gummed up in legal opposition, the removal of both statues has stalled. As a gesture and a promise, the city council has renamed the plots of land on which they stand Emancipation Park and Justice Park.

Things have changed in Charlottesville, I hear, have been changing everywhere, have never changed.

Figure 1:

A mundane white wall clock attached to an off-white wall. The minute hand is just before 8 and the hour hand is just before 11 and the second hand is on 7. The words "EQUITY" and "QUARTZ" are printed in the middle of the face. At the bottom left edge of the clock, four string-thin objects jut out.

If you squinted, they could be cracks in the wall. The middle two turn slightly inward at the tips.

Figure 2:

The clock has been removed to reveal a massive spider on the wall. The four jutting objects are the ends of its legs. You can look at Figure 1 again. The clock is back on the wall. But it's not the same.

HAIL SATAN

There are important issues on the table but all I can focus on is my ridiculous sticker. My Love bought it at a craft fair in Los Angeles. A sketch of an anthropomorphic hippo standing on his hind legs and wearing shorts, his chest emblazoned with a large pentagram and the words "HAIL SATAN." It screams me. I immediately stuck it to the cover of my teaching notebook, which I lay down in front of me at the start of an intense faculty meeting at the UVA summer writing program. It's July of 2017.

The Ku Klux Klan are rallying at the courthouse in Charlottesville this weekend. The program administrators want us to stay home. They aren't afraid of us confronting the Klan, they're afraid of us confronting the cops. There has already been a shakeup in the faculty—a late replacement—and they can't afford to have any of us detained and unable to teach. I'm going to be in a different city this weekend anyway; I have to be back in Los Angeles by August, when the larger, more foreboding fascist rally is set to occur.

I'm missing the crucial local moments. I have been for years.

Each summer of elementary school, my grandparents would take me and my brother to stay with them at their home in Germantown, Ohio, to give our parents short reprieves. Drawn by the word "German" in the name, Neo-Nazis would occasionally organize marches on the town's main street. I remember trying to explain to my brother why anyone would still be a Nazi, and coming up short. We stayed home and set booby traps for Gran, held Grandfather's boa constrictor while it tongued our cheekbones, hid in the skyscraping sunflowers by the garage.

Many in the city of Charlottesville advise caution that July, and organize alternate events to draw people away from Justice Park, where 50 or so Klan ooze out to defend the Jackson statue. This is the goofy Klan of yore—the kind that's easy for white people to distance themselves from. They don't get platforms to spew their hate in major media like the new alt-right variety does; they wear the standard robes, hold misspelled signs. Several hundred counter-protesters, including my dad and stepmom and many friends, arrive to surround and denounce them. Cops dressed in riot gear protect the cluster of Klan until they slink back to North Carolina. The counter-protest is declared unlawful and the riot cops shoot tear gas into the street. Over 20 people are arrested.[1] The administration was right to fear the cops.

Two days before, our faculty group deepens the conversation. The program is typically a welcoming, liberal, queer-friendly space. But some of the students will inevitably be from families that support the fascist president, some kids might already identify as conservatives. How can we make space for them?

Someone brings up the story of a student in the previous year whose parents disenrolled her from the program and came to take her home—a rare occurrence. She'd reported back to them how a teacher had played an offensive, anti-Christian song as part of a lesson. A story-song about a metal band, its closing refrain: "Hail Satan."

All I see is my satanic hippo. Ashamed of his irreverence, I cover the sticker with my hand. A sunflower blocking the light from above.

HH

On the morning of August 12, 2017, I open Instagram to a photograph of Dad. At the top left of the frame is the Lee statue, mainly horse, his head cropped out. Police barricades carve off empty park grass, a scattering of cops mill around. At the bottom right of the frame, Dad strolls. Four emoji arrows point to him, and overlayed text reads "this one guy was just walking by and didn't give off white supremacist vibes, fwiw."

I see the camera slung over Dad's back and I check the photos he's already posted: a man in the funeral home parking lot eyes an emptied state police truck. Its contents stand with their helmets and shields in warzone formation on the Downtown Mall. Counter-protesters assemble under a huge blown-up poster of the Obamas in an embrace.

I watch from a small brick apartment on the west coast, hunched over my pocket portal, frozen, moving only my frantic eyeballs and fingers. Images of the night before and the fascist attack that followed come in fragments, a strobe light turned on my former world.

The surprise assault on UVA Grounds, marchers chanting Nazi slogans, a small group of students and activists surrounded and brutalized under the statue of Jefferson.

Daylight. Upheld swastikas pass by the oldest standing synagogue in Virginia. Camouflaged militia members stalk the perimeter of Emancipation Park. Faith leaders form a line, linking arms. Antifascists arrive in force to protect them. The swarm of Nazis shout the n-word and, "fuck you faggots."

A sticker jumps out at me from a parked car. Two black letters in a black oval: "HH." I used to see it and think of my own initials, but it's a mundane stand-in for Hilton Head, part of a series of stickers that declare which southeast beach people go to on vacation, like "NH" or "OBX." Forgettable, from my childhood. After years of tracking white supremacist codes—hand signals, meme images—I see the two letters and read them as *Heil Hitler*. Nothing is innocuous today.

A man protects my friend's father from a Nazi charge with a makeshift flamethrower. Riot cops push the fascists from under Lee's statue, declaring the rally unlawful and rerouting them through the throngs of community counter-protesters to another site, the larger park named after the man who commissioned the Confederate statues.

Clear spray. Splashing milk. Purple smoke.

A silver car reverses across the Mall, its front bumper torn off and dragging. A red sneaker bounces out from underneath and lays still, a few feet from the silhouette of the man carrying Jefferson's head. From another angle, seconds before, the car plows into a crowd of people, the murderous impact captured by a local photographer.

Signs plead: Solidarity; Love; Stop. Inverted bodies, tossed in the air, a cyclone of water from burst bottles, sweat. The bare foot of a fallen person pressed against the dented bumper of a parked truck. Above, a maroon sticker reads: "No Man Stands So Tall, As When He Stoops to Help A Child."

The killer car is bereft of stickers—nothing fruity or pink or pixie, a blank canvas to be recruited. The make and model also used by cops. Unidentifiable and deadly.

I close my eyes. I call my family. I learn the name Heather Heyer.

When I return to town that winter, I'll stand on former 4th Street, now called Heather Heyer Way, in front of a shrine to her memory: flowers and rainbows of chalk honoring and thanking her, amplifying causes she stood and died for. I can't spot a car with the HH in the oval and not think of her, can't look at a gold star without thinking of the razing of Vinegar Hill, can't see a Rotunda sticker and see a simple allegiance—these connections are important and shouldn't be let go.

The statues are briefly covered in black shrouds, mourning those murdered in their name.

On the evening of August 12th, I sit at a backyard barbeque in Pasadena, feeling the ambient weight of nationwide focus on my hometown. A white couple talks loudly about Charlottesville. "I mean, I'm not surprised. I've been to Virginia," the woman says, "What do they call it, The Commonwealth? It's just . . . the South."

I get why people verbally adhere the label Charlottesville to the Unite the Right attack and murder. This helps them feel like the white supremacist evil only exists elsewhere, in some other place. Not where they happen to be.

The following day I join a march in downtown Los Angeles, beginning at City Hall and ending at the Metropolitan Detention Center, where ICE holds detainees. In front of me, a fellow protester hoists a sign that reads, "Stand with Charlottesville." I'm overwhelmed by the distance of a continent, no distance at all. I don't know how to react, so I take a picture. Soon, local stickers will be printed—"C'ville" in a heart, to show healing. A concert for unity will be organized. Speeches will be written, pleas for civility, asking, "how could this happen?" Saying, "this is not who we are." Charlottesville will be used as a shield, as a call-to-arms, as an excuse for unending oppression. To think the battle for the soul of America wasn't fought and won by white supremacy when the country was founded is to gravely misunderstand Charlottesville. There aren't enough "I Voted" stickers on Earth to cover up complicity.

When we reach the Detention Center, a march leader holds her megaphone upward and speaks in Spanish to the slatted prison windows above. She turns to us and speaks again. The word Charlottesville echoes.

Hearing the name, it hits me that I'm witnessing the afterlife of a place. Charlottesville has transubstantiated into multitudes, carried across the country to the minds of people who didn't give it a thought until the attack. It's still a town full of people and problems, but it will hold new meaning now, forever a signifier. Like America, like every other place on this planet. In Los Angeles, the monoliths of violent displacement and occupation come into sharper relief against the blue sky. Charlottesville is a tragedy, a testing ground, an inevitability, a teacher. And I'm from here.

NOTES

Mr. Yuk

1 Sally Ann Flecker, "It's Not Easy Being Green," *Pitt Med*, January 2003, https://www.pittmed.health.pitt.edu/story/it-s-not-easy-being-green

Gold Star

1 "About: History," Jefferson School City Center, accessed July, 2020, https://jeffersonschoolcitycenter.org/about/history/

2 "About Venable" Charlottesville City Schools, accessed July, 2020, http://charlottesvilleschools.org/venable/us/

3 Thomas Sellers, "Jefferson School Play," *The Reflector*, Issue 41, May 19, 1934, http://www2.vcdh.virginia.edu/afam/reflector/Play05.18.34.html

4 Graham Moomaw, "New markers honor Charlottesville 12 students," *The Daily Progress*, November 18, 2011,

Updated January 23, 2013, https://dailyprogress.com/news/new-markers-honor-charlottesville-students/article_097 17c60-3d0b-51c3-ba9c-a96ce3a1f46c.html

5   "John Hollis Bankhead II," Encyclopedia of Alabama, accessed July, 2020, http://encyclopediaofalabama.org/article/h-1424

6   Laura Smith, "In 1965, the city of Charlottesville demolished a thriving black neighborhood," *Timeline*, August 15, 2017, https://timeline.com/charlottesville-vinegar-hill-demolished-ba27b6ea69e1

7   "That World is Gone: Race and Displacement in a Small Southern Town," Field Studio Films, Accessed July, 2020, https://www.fieldstudiofilms.com/that-world-is-gone/

8   James Robert Saunders and Renae Nadine Shackelford, *Urban Renewal and the End of Black Culture in Charlottesville, Virginia: An Oral History of Vinegar Hill* (MacFarland, 1998).

9   Annie Waldman and Erica L. Green, "Charlottesville's Other Jim Crow Legacy: Separate and Unequal Education," *ProPublica / The New York Times*, October 16, 2018, https://www.propublica.org/article/charlottesville-other-jim-crow-legacy-separate-and-unequal-education

10   Seth Rosen, "City mindful of preserving Jefferson School legacy," *The Daily Progress*, July 6, 2007, Updated January 24, 2013, https://dailyprogress.com/news/city-mindful-of-preserving-jefferson-school-legacy/article_812fb768-661e-52ce-80cc-dcc653424a7d.html

11   "West Main Street, Press Kit," Rosalia Films, accessed July, 2020, https://rosaliafilms.com/films/west-main-street/press-kit/

Chiquita

1   Maria Iqbal, "Bodies, Brands, and Bananas: gender and race in the marketing of Chiquita Bananas," *Prandium -The Journal of Historical Studies*, Vol. 4, No. 1, Fall, 2015, http://jps.library.u toronto.ca/index.php/prandium/article/view/25691

2   Andrew Belonsky, "Today in Gay History: Tallulah Bankhead, Hoover's Favorite Diva," *Out Magazine,* January 31, 2014, https ://www.out.com/entertainment/today-gay-history/2014/01/31 /today-gay-history-tallulah-bankhead-hoover%E2%80%99s -favorite

Parental Advisory Explicit Content

1   Mathieu Deflem. "Popular Culture and Social Control: The Moral Panic on Music Labeling," *American Journal of Criminal Justice* 45(1):2-24, February, 2020.

2   Rania Aniftos, "A Timeline of Abuse Allegations Against Marilyn Manson," *Billboard*, February 8, 2021, https://www.bil lboard.com/articles/news/9523386/timeline-abuse-allegations-marilyn-manson

Rotunda

1   Kathleen Brunet, "Charlottesville Mall works for downtown," *The Free Lance-Star*, November 11, 1986, https://news.google.

com/newspapers?id=Ye0QAAAAIBAJ&sjid=F4wDAAAAIBAJ
&pg=4507%2C1962707

2 "Memorial to Enslaved Laborers," University of Virginia,
   accessed October, 2020, https://www2.virginia.edu/slaveryme
   morial/

3 Kellen Dunnavant, "Behind Her Eyes: The Story of Isabella
   Gibbons," *University of Virginia Office for Diversity, Equality,
   and Inclusion*, accessed October, 2020, https://vpdiversity.virgi
   nia.edu/isabella-gibbons

Anarchy

1 Susan Svrluga, "Charlottesville mourns a moving landmark,
   'Running Man,' after he is hit by an SUV," *The Washington Post*,
   December 31, 2015, https://www.washingtonpost.com/news/
   grade-point/wp/2015/12/31/charlottesville-mourns-a-moving-l
   andmark-running-man-after-he-is-hit-by-an-suv/

2 Kit Fox, "Locals Remember Charlottesville's 'Running Man,'"
   January 5, 2016, https://www.runnersworld.com/news/a20859
   405/locals-remember-charlottesvilles-running-man/

Blueberry

1 Matt Soniak, "How Does Scratch and Sniff Work?" *Mental
   Floss*, February 9, 2009, https://www.mentalfloss.com/article
   /20825/how-does-scratch-and-sniff-work

2 Svetlana Boym, *The Future of Nostalgia* (Basic Books, 2001).

Death to the Pixies

1 "Charlottesville High School reopened today after defiant students were. . ." *UPI,* March 6, 1984, https://www.upi.com/Archives/1984/03/06/Charlottesville-High-School-reopened-today-after-defiant-students-were/9585447397200/

2 "Woman claiming to be Anastasia Romanov arrives in the U.S." *History.com*, accessed August, 2020, https://www.history.com/this-day-in-history/anastasia-arrives-in-the-united-states

3 William O. Tucker Jr, "Jack & Anna: Remembering the czar of Charlottesville eccentrics," *The Hook*, July 5, 2007, http://www.readthehook.com/86004/cover-jack-amp-anna-remembering-czar-charlottesville-eccentrics

4 "'Anastasia' abducted from Charlottesville hospital on this day in 1983," *The Daily Progress*, November 29, 2017, https://dailyprogress.com/125yearsofprogress/anastasia-abducted-from-charlottesville-hospital-this-day-in-1983/article_5e38d7a2-d48b-11e7-b5fe-0bcb4c84f922.html

Pink Circle

1 Raphael Rubinstein, "Bartleby on Carmine Street," *The Brooklyn Rail*, July-August, 2016, https://brooklynrail.org/2016/07/fiction/bartleby-on-carmine-street

2 Steven Ward, "Whatever happened to rock critic Paul Nelson,"
RockCritics.com, March 2000, https://rockcritics.com/2013/01
/28/from-the-archives-interview-with-paul-nelson/

Heart

1 Keelin McDonell, "The Shape of My Heart," *Slate*, February 13,
2007, https://slate.com/news-and-politics/2007/02/where-does-
the-ubiquitous-valentine-s-heart-shape-come-from.html

2 Ibid.

Fire Dancer

1 Damani Harrison and Mark Grabowski, "The masters: Seven
local CDs," *The Hook*, June 24, 2004, http://www.readthehook
.com/95334/cover-masters-seven-local-cds

2 Chuck Salter, "Way behind the music," *Fast Company*, February
1, 2007, https://www.fastcompany.com/58508/way-behind-
music

3 Marissa Hermanson, "It's Capshaw's world," *C-VILLE Weekly*,
April 27, 2004, https://www.c-ville.com/Its_Capsaws_world

4 Tim Marcin, "Dave Matthews Band Dropped 800 Pounds of
Human Waste on Chicago Sightseers 14 Years Ago Today,"
Newsweek, August 8, 2018, https://www.newsweek.com/dave-

matthews-band-dropped-800-pounds-feces-chicago-sightseers
-14-years-ago-1064129

Be Nice to Me I Gave Blood Today

1   Maggie L. Shaw, "FDA's Revised Blood Donation Guidance for
    Gay Men Still Courts Controversy," *The American Journal for
    Managed Care*, April 4, 2020, https://www.ajmc.com/view/fdas
    -revised-blood-donation-guidance-for-gay-men-still-courts-co
    ntroversy

Are You Triggered?

1   Paul Duggan, "Charlottesville's Confederate statues still stand—
    and still symbolize a racist legacy," *The Washington Post*, August
    10, 2019, https://www.washingtonpost.com/history/2019/08
    /10/charlottesvilles-confederate-statues-still-stand-still-symbo
    lize-racist-past/

2   W.E.B. Du Bois, "The Perfect Vacation," *The Crisis*, August,
    1931.

3   Joe Heim, "Va. cities and counties increasingly want to make
    Lee-Jackson-King Day history," *The Washington Post*, January
    11, 2018, https://www.washingtonpost.com/local/va-cities-and
    -counties-increasingly-want-to-make-lee-jackson-day-history/
    2018/01/11/adfea9d8-f23b-11e7-b390-a36dc3fa2842_story.html

4 Jacey Fortin, "The Statue at the Center of Charlottesville's Storm," *The New York Times*, August 13, 2017, https://www.nytimes.com/2017/08/13/us/charlottesville-rally-protest-statue.html

5 W.E.B. Du Bois, "Postscript," *The Crisis*, March, 1928.

Hail Satan

1 Hawes Spencer and Matt Stevens, "23 Arrested and Tear Gas Deployed After a K.K.K. Rally in Virginia," July 8, 2017, https://www.nytimes.com/2017/07/08/us/kkk-rally-charlottesville-robert-e-lee-statue.html

ACKNOWLEDGEMENTS

Ceaseless love to my family, for their support of my ongoing identity, and to Merkel, a brilliant and generous collaborator and companion.

Thanks to my classmates in the Charlottesville City school system, and to all my teachers, guides, and inspirations, including Rita Dove, Julian Bond, Mark Tramontin, Jenny Johnson, Branden Jacobs-Jenkins, Mady Schutzman, Matias Viegener, Maggie Nelson, Janet Sarbanes, Ashaki M Jackson, Claudia Rankine, Robin Coste Lewis, Kenyatta AC Hinkle, Douglas Kearney, and Margo Figgins.

Thanks to Christopher Schaberg, Ian Bogost, Haaris Naqvi, and everyone at Bloomsbury, for believing in my vision, and to Ryan Heffington, Other Half Brewing, Court Street Grocers, Harold Budd, and Emahoy Tsegué-Maryam Guèbrou, for getting me through this pandemic writing process.

My deepest gratitude and admiration to Zyahna Bryant, Wes Bellamy, Tanesha Hudson, Nikuyah Walker, Cornel West, Seth Wispelwey, Jamelle Bouie, Jordy Yager, Molly Conger, DeAndre Harris, Emily Gorcenski, Corey Long,

Susan Bro, Heather Heyer, and anyone fighting fascism and working to dismantle white supremacy, at whatever stage of education or engagement.

Special thanks to The Jefferson School African American Heritage Center, where all royalties from *Sticker* will be directly donated.

This book is for Katy.

INDEX

OBJECTLESSONS

Cross them all off your list.

TV

9781501362521

blackface

9781501374012

hyphen

9781501373909

spacecraft

9781501375804

football

9781501367069

perfume

9781501367144

Burger by Carol J. Adams

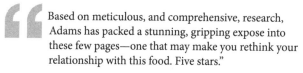

Based on meticulous, and comprehensive, research, Adams has packed a stunning, gripping expose into these few pages—one that may make you rethink your relationship with this food. Five stars."

San Francisco Book Review

Adams would seem the least likely person to write about hamburgers with her philosophically lurid antipathy to carnivory. But if the point is to deconstruct this iconic all-American meal, then she is the woman for the job."

Times Higher Education

It's tempting to say that *Burger* is a literary meal that fills the reader's need, but that's the essence of Adams' quick, concise, rich exploration of the role this meat (or meatless) patty has played in our lives."

PopMatters

High Heel by **Summer Brennan**

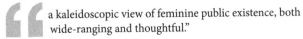 a kaleidoscopic view of feminine public existence, both
wide-ranging and thoughtful."

Jezebel

Brennan makes the case that high heels are an apt
metaphor for the ways in which women have been
hobbled in their mobility. She also tackles the
relationship between beauty and suffering, highlighting
the fraught nature of reclaiming objects defined under
patriarchy for feminism."

Paste Magazine

From Cinderella's glass slippers to Carrie Bradshaw's
Manolo Blahniks, Summer Brennan deftly analyzes
one of the world's most provocative and sexualized
fashion accessories . . . Whether you see high heels
as empowering or a submission to patriarchal gender
roles (or land somewhere in between), you'll likely
never look at a pair the same way again after reading
High Heel."

Longreads

Brennan's book, written in very small sections, is short, but powerful enough to completely change your world view."

Refinery29

In *High Heel*, the wonderful Summer Brennan embraces a slippery, electric conundrum: Does the high heel stand for oppression or power? . . . *High Heel* elevates us, keeps us off balance, and sharpens the point."

The Philadelphia Inquirer

Hood by Alison Kinney

Provocative and highly informative, Alison Kinney's *Hood* considers this seemingly neutral garment accessory and reveals it to be vexed by a long history of violence, from the Grim Reaper to the KKK and beyond—a history we would do well to address, and redress. Readers will never see hoods the same way again."

Sister Helen Prejean, author of
Dead Man Walking

Hood is searing. It describes the historical properties of the hood, but focuses on this object's modern-day connotations. Notably, it dissects the racial fear evoked by young black men in hoodies, as shown by the senseless killings of unarmed black males. It also touches on U.S. service members' use of hoods to mock and torture prisoners at Abu Ghraib. Hoods can represent the (sometimes toxic) power of secret affiliations, from monks to Ku Klux Klan members. And clearly they can also be used by those in power to dehumanize others. In short, *Hood* does an excellent job of unspooling the many faces of hoods."

Book Riot

[*Hood*] is part of a series entitled Object Lessons, which looks at 'the hidden lives of ordinary things' and which are all utterly 'Fridge Brilliant' (defined by TV Tropes as an experience of sudden revelation, like the light coming on when you open a refrigerator door). . . . In many ways *Hood* isn't about hoods at all. It's about what—and who—is under the hood. It's about the hooding, the hooders and the hoodees . . . [and] identity, power and politics. . . . Kinney's book certainly reveals the complex history of the hood in America."

London Review of Books

Personal Stereo by
Rebecca Tuhus-Dubrow

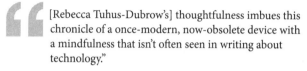

[Rebecca Tuhus-Dubrow's] thoughtfulness imbues this chronicle of a once-modern, now-obsolete device with a mindfulness that isn't often seen in writing about technology."

Pitchfork (named one of *Pitchfork's* favorite books of 2017)

After finishing *Personal Stereo*, I found myself wondering about the secret lives of every object around me, as if each device were whispering, 'Oh, I am much so more than meets the eye' . . . Tuhus-Dubrow is a master researcher and synthesizer. . . . *Personal Stereo* is a joy to read."

Los Angeles Review of Books

Personal Stereo is loving, wise, and exuberant, a moving meditation on nostalgia and obsolescence. Rebecca Tuhus-Dubrow writes as beautifully about Georg Simmel and Allan Bloom as she does about Jane Fonda and Metallica. Now I understand why I still own the taxicab-yellow Walkman my grandmother gave me in 1988."

Nathaniel Rich, author of
Odds Against Tomorrow

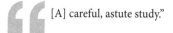

[A] careful, astute study."

The Wire

Souvenir by Rolf Potts

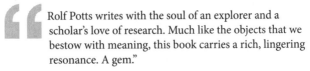

Rolf Potts writes with the soul of an explorer and a
scholar's love of research. Much like the objects that we
bestow with meaning, this book carries a rich, lingering
resonance. A gem."

Andrew McCarthy, actor, director, and author of
The Longest Way Home (2013)

Souvenir, a sweet new book by Rolf Potts, is a little
gem (easily tucked into a jacket pocket) filled with big
insights . . . *Souvenir* explores our passions for such
possessions and why we are compelled to transport
items from one spot to another."

Forbes

A treasure trove of . . . fascinating deep dives into
the history of travel keepsakes . . . Potts walks us
through the origins of some of the most popular
vacation memorabilia, including postcards and the
still confoundedly ubiquitous souvenir spoons. He
also examines the history of the more somber side
of mementos, those depicting crimes and tragedies.
Overall, the book, as do souvenirs themselves, speaks
to the broader issues of time, memory, adventure, and
nostalgia."

The Boston Globe

Veil by Rafia Zakaria

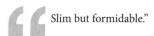

Slim but formidable."

London Review of Books

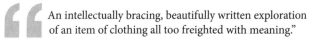

Rafia Zakaria's *Veil* shifts the balance away from white secular Europe toward the experience of Muslim women, mapping the stereotypical representations of the veil in Western culture and then reflecting, in an intensely personal way, on the many meanings that the veil can have for the people who wear it . . . [*Veil* is] useful and important, providing needed insight and detail to deepen our understanding of how we got here—a necessary step for thinking about whether and how we might be able to move to a better place."

The Nation

An intellectually bracing, beautifully written exploration of an item of clothing all too freighted with meaning."

Molly Crabapple, artist, journalist, and author of *Drawing Blood* (2015)